12 Simple Tools to Su

TOOLS FOR
Extraordinary
LIVING

THE SNOOZE BUTTON SESSIONS

KERRY B. FISHER

Library of Congress Cataloging-in-Publication Data
Names: Fisher, Kerry, Author
Title: *12 SIMPLE TOOLS FOR EXTRAORDINARY LIVING: THE SNOOZE BUTTON SESSIONS*
LCCN xxxxxxxxxx

ISBN 978-1-958165-00-3 (Softcover)
ISBN 978-1-958165-01-0(Hardcover)
ISBN 978-1-958165-02-7(eBook)

Nonfiction, Mind, Body & Spirit, Self-Help, Personal Development

The first step towards getting somewhere is to decide that you are not going to stay where you are.

—J.P. Morgan

Dedicated to Vishen Lakhiani, founder of Mindvalley.

Thank you for inspiring me, uplifting me, helping me to believe in myself and educating me. It was you who gave me the idea that maybe I could be everything I've dreamed of being, that maybe I could have the life of my dreams.

My life utterly changed when I began my Mindvalley journey, and I owe you my everlasting gratitude for your vision; your dream of a better world.

This book would have remained in my computer forever if it weren't for you. I appreciate you. I admire you. I thank you.

XO Kerry

CONTENTS

If you come to a fork in the road, take it.

—Yogi Berra

A MESSAGE FROM KERRY:
HOW THE SNOOZE BUTTON
TRANSFORMED MY LIFE

L et me take you back to a moment that changed my life... I was in Israel hiking with my family. We came to a beautiful clearing. There were trees arranged in a perfect circle around a giant space covered in pine needles. Birds were chirping, the sun was filtering down. Sounds were muffled. A sense of mystery hovered in the air. I sat down in the middle of the clearing, gazing at the trees around me. There was a feeling of expectancy in the air. I felt like I had been there before. The sense of *déjà vu* was strong.

Suddenly, I had a vivid flashback, and I was transported back in time. It was as if I were watching a movie. I could see everything in perfect detail. In my mind's eye, I could see the younger Kerry, the younger me, sitting in the middle of a clearing just like the one I was in. There she was, alone in the woods, writing furiously in her journal. I had flashed back to a scene from my early 20s when I was living on a kibbutz in Israel. Those were tumultuous years for me because I had dropped out of college in my senior year to travel the world. Upon reflection, it was not the best planning, I know, but back then, it seemed like a fantastic idea, a perfect plan—drop out of school and then drop out of life to become a world traveler. Nobody ever said young adults have great reasoning skills and I, for one, certainly didn't!

The younger version of me had gone to Israel to find myself by purposely losing myself. I had given away everything I owned except for my series of Hermann Hesse books, and I hit the road with a backpack, $500, and a thirst for adventure. I was planning to completely drop out, no contact with anyone or anything for the entire year. No credit cards, no cellphone; it was just me and the world. Ok, and a nice pair of heels. Perfect adventure travel attire, right? I wanted to *live* my life fully; I wanted to explore the world. I was always searching back then—searching, searching, ever searching—looking for the meaning of life.

I've always been a dreamer and a deep thinker. From my earliest memories, I questioned why some people have so much while others have so little. It seemed to me there were enough resources, they just weren't distributed properly. I never quite understood why we couldn't all "just get along." I was positive the world would be a better place if everyone just learned to share. Communal living was exactly what I envisioned. It was a dream come true for someone like me. Working together, eating together, living together—isn't this the way life was supposed to be? It certainly seemed that way for me. So when I learned that a kibbutz was an experiment in communal living, I had to try it. Off to Israel I went and onto the kibbutz I moved.

On the kibbutz, we worked and took classes in exchange for room, board, and travel throughout Israel. Whenever I wasn't working on the kibbutz, I would spend time in nature. I loved to hike to a clearing right outside the kibbutz and ponder the great mysteries of the universe. I would sit and write in my journal, detailing all my hopes and dreams. This is exactly what I was doing on that day so many years before. I was sitting, writing in my journal, and imagining what my perfect future would look like.

As I sat there 30 years later, I was swept away by the vividness of the memory. I flashed back to what I had written that day: Get married to a smart, kind man, have lots of kids, a big house with enough land for animals and a garden. Become an expert chef. There would be dinner on the table every single night, and we would eat as a family. I would have a job I loved. The current me could see it all so clearly; it was like my younger self was sitting next to me, and I was reading the journal as she wrote it. Those things I was writing long ago seemed so out of reach to the 22-year-old version of me. I wasn't sure how I could go from the young woman I was to the woman I wanted to become.

Yet, here I was, many years later, all grown up, and I realized in a flash that all my dreams had come true. I was looking at my husband and my five kids. I was traveling with the very family I had once yearned to have. I had a job I loved. Everything I had written in that journal so many years prior had come true. Talk about a surreal, out of body moment; it was like the adult Kerry was standing behind the young Kerry, reading her journal and saying, "Check, check, check." In a flash, I realized that although I had acquired everything I had dreamed of all those years earlier, I still felt a deep yearning inside. How could this be, I wondered? Why was I so unfulfilled? If every single dream I had once dreamed had come to pass, why was I still feeling like something was missing? Why wasn't I happy? I sat in that clearing pondering how mysterious life truly is. I wondered, truly wondered, what was missing?

Then, it hit me. I knew what I had to do... I had to start dreaming again! That was the only way to recreate my life anew, to become the next grandest version of who I wanted to be. I needed to make a new list, dream new dreams—become a new me.

As soon as we made it back to the hotel, I sat down and wrote furiously. I began writing down anything and everything I dreamed of. I didn't hold back. I dreamed the most daring, glorious life I could imagine, no holds barred. I allowed myself to write down anything and everything that popped into my head. I was writing so fast; I didn't even know what I was writing.

When I was done, I sat back, satisfied, and looked at what I had written: Spend more time with my kids and husband; spend more time outdoors; expand my career; write the book I always wanted to write; help more people; become an international speaker; enjoy more adventures; buy a beach house. It went on and on and on. As I stared at the list, I started to think the entire thing was silly. How was I going to do this? The doubts poured in.

I sat there, staring at my new dream-list and the doubts continued. Then I heard a voice. (No, I wasn't going crazy; it was my own voice.) The voice was from deep down inside me. The voice I never really listened to much because I was so busy doing the right thing, being responsible, and adulting like crazy.

The voice said, "You can do anything you put your mind to. Once you decide, you will figure out how to make it work. Look at all you have accomplished until now. Just make the commitment and move forward." I made the decision in that moment to commit to accomplishing everything I dreamed of. I would create an epic life—the life of my dreams!

A few months after I had made my dream list, I made an effort to create some changes. But it was *hard*. I was resisting. My life was *busy*! I had no time for dream fulfillment. Most days I was just trying to get by—working, cooking, cleaning, chauffeuring my children around, sports, activities, laundry, pets... I had a lot of excuses. Then, something happened that truly changed my life.

One morning, the alarm clock sounded. I went to hit the snooze button, as usual. Something stopped me, a thought. Robin Sharma's thought, "To get the results that only 5% of the people get, you have to be willing to do what only 5% of the people are willing to do." I decided to hit the snooze but instead of going back to sleep, I meditated. When the alarm clock rang again, I turned it off, got up, and started my day. I didn't think too much about it, I didn't know my entire *life* had just changed. But it had!

That day went really smoothly; it was so easy. I was calm, collected, relaxed all day long. Nothing could get to me. Not the guy cutting me off on the road, not the person who took my spot in the parking lot, not the student who didn't like my class, not my kids acting like kids do. I was unperturbed. No matter what happened, I was completely centered. I thought to myself, "What's different? Why is everything so easy today?" Then I remembered that I had meditated in the morning. Was that it?

I told my husband about this snooze technique, and he tried using it. After trying it out for just one day, my husband told me it had been one of the best days of his life. This was interesting considering he had worked a full ten-hour day and then came home to the pandemonium that was our home. My husband grew quiet. We sat there, staring at each other, thrilled that we had found something so simple that could change the quality of our entire day. We agreed that we would continue doing this each day and maybe stretch or do yoga too. And that is what we did. Each day we would awaken and do our practices. And it was a true game changer.

I started to feel really, really *good!* I felt accomplished. Each day, before I even started my day, I had wins, serious wins. The simple act of getting up instead of snoozing helped me to create a healthy morning routine. This calm start to my day stood in marked contrast to waiting until the last moment to leap out of bed trying to catch up with the day.

My life was changing, my body was changing, and my mind was changing. I was centered. I was happy. My entire life was moving in an entirely different direction than ever before. Life became easy. And when life becomes easy, it frees up a lot of time to craft the life of dreams. So, that is exactly what I did.

At this same time, I began journaling daily. During one of my morning journaling sessions, I remembered that when I was a young girl, my greatest wish was to become a writer. I used to write poetry in my room when I was little. I knew I would be a writer one day. I didn't *think* it, I *knew* it. That was my life's path. As a young girl, I wrote all the time, but I never showed anyone my writing. Life had other plans for me, but it wasn't too late I decided. It's never too late.

The next day, during my morning snooze session, I started writing. It felt good; it felt right. I never planned to write an entire book, and by no means was I planning on getting my book published. Writing was just for me. One day, I wrote the outline for this book, and I began to think that this technique that I had accidentally stumbled upon had the capacity to create real, measurable change in people's lives. It was a simple way to do small, daily acts of greatness which would then create new habits. it was a simple method to create new ways of thinking that would give the space for people to contemplate things they want to change in their lives.

I didn't just write about a method to create real, positive change, I lived it. The more I incorporated these morning practices into my life, the better my life got. My conviction grew that this could help other people. I started to teach these ideas to my students and then, one day, I taught an entire class on using the snooze button to meditate, journal, exercise or read. I was teaching my theories. It was happening! And the best part was that people were telling me that it was changing their lives. They were finally meditating or exercising or journaling. It worked for them just as it had worked for me! And it was easy.

As I taught the snooze button ideas, they became a lot more real to me, everything became clear. I asked for feedback from my students, I asked them to keep me up to date on their progress. I began using this material everywhere I worked. I incorporated the ideas into my work with corporate clients, teaching them stress reduction. I used the snooze button technique when I was teaching kids mindfulness. It was even applicable when I taught peak performance to athletic teams.

Life became magical. I became a better teacher, and my students were getting better results. I was in flow. The most amazing part of it all was that these concepts were helpful to EVERYONE! As my business expanded, so did my belief that these ideas could help people transform their lives. The ideas evolved, and this book is the result of that evolution.

What you have in your hands is a blueprint for creating and maintaining positive change in your life. This book is about taking action. This book is about getting results. It's a no-nonsense, no bullshit guide to creating change and transformation. The entire book is based on the idea that "big change starts small." We can create lasting, effective change in our lives by simply changing small things day by day.

It is said that "The journey of a thousand miles begins with one step." It is my wish that this book be that first step for you.

XO Kerry

You can always begin again.

—Sharon Salzburg

INTRODUCTION

D id you ever notice that nobody ever gives you an entire book on how to live a great life, an epic life, the life of your dreams? Would you agree that, in life, we are told what to do, we are even shown how to do it, but the general prescription for life that is offered may not always apply to everyone?

As children, we are taught that all we have to do is make our bed, keep our room clean, listen to our parents, work hard in school, and everything will turn out fine. As we get a little older, we are told to go to college, listen to our professors, work hard, keep making our bed, and everything will be fine. We become adults and take on countless responsibilities. In addition, we are told to work hard, be reliable, listen to our boss and while we are at it, keep making our bed, and everything will work out fine.

So we do all the things we are supposed to do—work, move forward, aim towards our goals. And yet, we still feel unfulfilled, as if something is missing. Then, we think to ourselves, "Is this it?" Is this what life is all about? Have you ever had a moment like that, where you find yourself wondering why you are even on this earth? I call it "a dark night of the soul moment."

The most important days of our lives are the day we are born and the day we find out why we were born. When you experience your dark night of the soul moment, you may very well be discovering why you were born. Even though you may feel empty and purposeless in that moment, if you pay close attention, you will realize that you are being granted the exact opening you need to realize your true purpose on earth. During this time, those moments can make you feel empty. But years later, you will find that you are beyond grateful for that experience.

> *The dark night of the soul comes just before revelation.*
> *When everything is lost, and all seems darkness,*
> *then comes the new life and all that is needed.*
> —Joseph Campbell

Those are the moments when every single thing in your life can change. In fact, this book is a result of one of those moments. This book was written with you in mind. I am living my purpose by bringing this book to you and sharing the practices that helped me create the life I dreamed of. It is my greatest wish that this book provides you with the tools you need to live your purpose.

I am rooting for you.

Does your story inspire you?
If not, it's time to change it.

—Apostolos Pliassas

CHAPTER 1

THE SNOOZE BUTTON SESSIONS TECHNIQUE

The journey of a thousand miles
begins with one step.
—Lao Tzu

The definition of snooze is to take a nap. In most Western cultures, the term snooze is often associated with the alarm clock. Once our alarm clock sounds, we have the option of pressing the snooze button. This temporarily turns your alarm off for a few minutes (snooze time) before the alarm sounds again. Typically, people use snooze time to squeeze in a few more moments of rest before getting out of bed for the day. If you cherish your sleep, then your snooze time is precious to you. But what if there was another use for snooze time? What if there was a way to use the snooze to change your life?

I would like to introduce you to a simple, yet effective, way to use the snooze button to your benefit. It's called a Snooze Button Session. A

Snooze Button Session is a way to use something you are already doing, pressing the snooze button, and use it to start your day off right and maybe, just maybe, even change your life. You might be thinking, "How could pressing the snooze button change my life?" Well, by hitting the snooze button and doing one of the incredible practices you will find in this book, you will be taking care of your body, your mind, and your spirit. You are adding conscious attention to your day. As with anything in life, when you add more conscious attention to a process, the nature of it changes completely.

Whether you are someone who doesn't use the snooze button on your clock at all or someone who cherishes your snooze time, we want to change the way you think about your snooze button. For the sake of this book, think of a Snooze Button Session as an active snooze. It's a way to take advantage of the time between pressing the snooze button and the sound of the second alarm. Instead of going back to sleep, you are going to use your alarm clock as a way to incorporate healthy habits into your life without taking any extra time from your day.

What makes the snooze button so effective as a way to build habits is that it is something you may already naturally do. In this way, pressing the snooze button becomes the anchor to whatever practice you add to it. This connection makes it easier to remember to do the additional activity. This is the core principle behind a concept called habit stacking (more on this later).

In each of the coming chapters, you will find a new practice along with different techniques you can use when approaching it. Try any technique that feels appropriate for you and truly practice it for a few days before trying a new one. In order to make this journey as accessible (and fun) for you as possible, all we ask is that you try one practice/technique per week. Usually, when we try something new, it feels weird and even uncomfortable. So, by sticking with each practice for at least a week, there will be less of a likelihood that you quit early. Additionally, this will give you some time to incorporate the practice into your normal routine.

This book is designed to help you easily bring these practices into your daily life. The exercises included in this book are formatted to be used after pressing the snooze button on your alarm. By trying one technique each week, you will start to see which ones are keepers and which ones simply don't work for you. With practice and consistency, you will have a very clear idea of which techniques work for you, and which don't. As you begin to understand why some techniques work and others do not, you will be learning a lot about yourself and you will also be creating a routine that works for you. That is the beauty of this system—it can be tailored to your needs and preferences. Simply start by doing the first practice and try it for a few days or even a week. Then, move on to the next practice and try that one. Eventually, you will find some that are great for you and others that simply do not resonate with you. That is the point. You want to try all the different practices and then decide which works for you.

It is important to note that simply reading through this book will introduce you to some great techniques for a better life, but in order to create real and sustained positive changes in your life, use this book as a workbook. This means that if you put in the (totally relaxing and enjoyable) "work," you will see massive positive changes in your life. If you don't actually do the exercises, you will miss some of the power of the techniques.

For now, to get started, all I ask is that you dedicate one snooze interval each day to practicing the technique of the week before moving on to the next one. Truthfully, if all you end up with is a five-minute meditation or breath exercise each morning, you are already well on your way to a calmer, more relaxed lifestyle.

Let's snooze, shall we?

> *The way to get started is to quit talking and begin doing.*
> —Walt Disney

*Breathing is the greatest
pleasure in life.*

—Giovanni Papin

CHAPTER 2

BREATHING

To breathe properly is to live properly.
—Robin Sharma

I remember taking Lamaze classes when I was pregnant with my first child. I thought it was very funny and a little silly to think that breathing would help me get through the pain of labor, but I dutifully took the class.

When I went into labor, I was in a lot of pain, then I remembered the breath classes I had taken. I started to concentrate on my breath, and I was amazed that not only did the pain recede, but I also felt calmer and more peaceful after just one round of breath. It worked! I decided to study breath after that and found that one of the easiest ways to change your state was by changing your breath.

I was convinced. Ever since that day, I've been doing breathwork exercises daily. They were so helpful to me and to my emotional state that I decided to dive deep into the world of breathwork and to learn everything I could about the way the breath affects the body. Eventually I began to teach these techniques to others and the effects were, dare I say it, breathtaking. They are truly a game-changer.

How often do you stop and pay attention to your breathing throughout the day? Unfortunately, most of us rarely stop to pay attention to our breathing. Since breathing is such a vital part of life, let's take some time to consider why you should pay more close attention to your breath.

> *Breathe.*
> *Let go.*
> *And remind yourself that this very moment is the*
> *only one you know you have for sure.*
> —Oprah Winfrey

Breathing is a natural function of the human body. For thousands of years, Eastern cultures have recognized the importance of the breath. In the West, breath practices have come into the mainstream as practices like yoga and martial arts have become more and more popular. The importance of the breath is finally being recognized around the world as a constantly renewable source of personal energy.

The breath has long been a part of our language. Think about phrases we use to express a happy feeling like, "it was like a breath of fresh air." Or when we're relieved, we say, "I breathed a sigh of relief." When we want someone to keep our secrets, we say, "don't breathe a word about this." When we're fearful, we say, "I couldn't catch my breath," or "it felt like someone was breathing down my neck." And of course, when we're in awe we say, "it was breathtaking," or "it took my breath away." We are unconsciously aware of our breath. The point of this practice is to become consciously aware of our breath.

We typically breathe automatically, but the cool thing about the breath is that it can also be a voluntary activity. The breath is the one function that we can actually control if we choose to control it. Isn't that amazing?

But why would you want to control your breath?

One of the main reasons that you might want to learn to control your breath is that you can actually change your state if you change your breathing. You can change your physical state, your emotional state, your mental state and perhaps, even your spiritual state. Your breath is intricately connected to all of these areas. Here is where the true magic is: As you learn to harness your breath, you will find that not only does your breath affect your state but that it is a two-way system. That's right! Your breath affects your state but your state also affects your breath. Pretty amazing, isn't it?

Breath is the bridge which connects life to consciousness,
which unites your body to your thoughts.
Whenever your mind becomes scattered,
use your breath as the means to take
hold of your mind again.
—Thich Nhat Hanh

Your breath serves as an extraordinary information system. It is always communicating with you. When you're happy, your breath naturally feels free, open, and expansive. When you're frightened, you usually tense up, and your breath becomes constricted. Your breath can help you to pay attention to how you are feeling and what you are experiencing at any given moment. Your breath can inform your life and teach you about yourself.

As we discussed above, the breath naturally follows our physical and emotional state. This means even when your thoughts are expressing one message to you, just by tuning into your breathing, you may discover something totally different. So paying attention to the breath can help you understand yourself on a much deeper level.

Breathing enables your body to get the energy it needs to power your cells. When you breathe in, you bring oxygen into your lungs. The oxygen-rich blood from your lungs goes through the pulmonary veins and then into the left side of your heart and then the blood is pumped throughout your body, bringing the oxygen-rich red blood cells into all the cells of your body. Your cells use the oxygen to make energy. And here's the best part, the magic that happens. As your cells convert oxygen into energy, carbon monoxide is created as a by-product of the process and this carbon monoxide is sent back out through the bloodstream back to the heart and then the lungs and finally, it's exhaled. Pretty cool, right?

Here's one of the most incredible aspects of our breath. You see, humans need oxygen in order to power our cells and create energy. Plants need carbon monoxide in order to power their life processes. And this is where we see the magic. The undesirable by-product of human breathing is carbon monoxide, the very thing that plants need to use to create their energy. Humans exhale what the plants need to survive. It goes even further though. Plants release oxygen into the air around them because oxygen is an undesirable by-product of their processes and oxygen is an essential element needed by humans to create energy for their systems. Humans and plants are quite literally exchanging the life force they need to survive. This is how powerfully connected we are to the world around us. Makes you want to get a few more plants in your house, right?

Let's become even more enchanted with our breath. Check this out: We breathe about 16 breaths per minute. This is 960 breaths per hour. Which means we breathe about 23,000 breaths per day. Think about that! Awesome, right? We breathe over 8,400,000 breaths per year. Breath is vitally important yet we often simply ignore it. Imagine if you brought some focus and attention to some of these breaths. Imagine if you allow your breath to become your anchor when you feel stressed, your comfort when you feel overwhelmed, your source of power when you need it. That, my friends, is the power of the breath. It can nourish your physical, mental, emotional, and spiritual state.

If this wasn't enough to convince you of how amazing the breath is, then maybe this is. You can go three weeks without food, you can go three days without water, you can go three hours in a harsh environment without proper gear yet you can only go three minutes without breath. Three minutes. You can only go three minutes without breath. Breath is that important. Breath is arguably the single most important thing we need to survive and thrive.

There are a lot of new and exciting studies coming out that show just how important the breath really is. A 2016 study found that a neural circuit in the brainstem plays a role in adjusting breathing rhythm which in turn affects the emotional state. The study found that using slow controlled breathing actually decreases activity in this circuit while fast erratic breathing increases activity in this pathway. By controlling the breath, you can regulate this circuit. Using simple breath exercises can help you to control your emotions. Perhaps even more exciting is that another study, also done in 2016, showed that our breathing patterns actually affects our memory.

Another powerful study done by researchers at Trinity College of Neuroscience and Global Brain Health Institute found that breathing affects a natural brain chemical messenger called noradrenaline. Noradrenaline is released into your body when you are in a state of increased focus and it serves to enhance your attention to detail. This promotes the growth of new neural connections and improves overall brain health.

The researchers measured the breathing patterns of participants and found that those people who were able to focus well on a demanding task were better able to synchronize their breathing patterns and attention while those who were not able to focus well had inconsistent breathing patterns. This means that your breath affects your attention and your attention affects your breath. This study indicates that you can improve your attention span by regulating your breath.

There are so many benefits to learning and using a breath practice. Check out the list below for more benefits.

BENEFITS OF BREATHING

Intentional Breathing Improves:
- focus/concentration

- alertness
- sleep
- level of peace/relaxation
- immunity
- level of energy
- digestion

Intentional Breathing Reduces:
- stress
- anxiety
- depression
- brain fog
- blood pressure
- fatigue
- pain

Inhale the future, exhale the past.
—Unknown

The following exercises are what are known as breathing exercises. Engaging in breathing exercises is an ideal way to strengthen your connection with your breath. These exercises will positively alter your emotional and mental state. As you get better at paying attention to your breath, you can start doing these exercises a few times throughout the day to monitor and manage your state. Notice how you feel each time you practice one of these breath exercises.

Note: If this is your first time doing breathing exercises, some of these exercises may cause you to experience new and unusual feelings in your body. Make sure you are practicing these exercises in a safe and comfortable environment. Ideally, just sit up and practice them in bed.

Pay close attention to how you are feeling. If you feel dizzy or begin to feel anxious or more stressed, then please stop the exercise and allow yourself to go back to your typical breathing. You can try the exercise again once you feel better, or you can try a different exercise. With practice, your body will begin to get used to the different methods of breathing.

The goal of this exercise, and with all of the practices in this book, is to simply observe yourself to see what works and what doesn't work for you. You want to find the practices that nourish you and make you feel good. If a practice doesn't feel good, move on from it for now. This is your opportunity to learn about yourself and find what works best for you.

Feelings come and go like clouds in a windy sky.
Conscious breathing is my anchor.
—Thich Nhat Hanh

THE BREATHING EXERCISES

Ok, here we go. We are about to embark upon our very first Snooze Session. Tomorrow morning, you will hit the snooze button and practice one of the exercises below. Are you ready to change your life? Let's do it.

Note: For each of the following exercises, unless noted otherwise, begin by sitting in a comfortable position with a straight back. Close your eyes to increase your level of relaxation.

EXERCISE 1: BREATH AWARENESS

By bringing your attention to your breath, you can increase your level of awareness and calm. This exercise simply requires you to bring your attention to the tip of your nose, then notice your breath as it comes in and goes out of your body. That is all there is to it.

PRACTICE

- Notice how you are feeling.
- Bring your attention to the tip of your nose in order to focus your mind.
- Take a deep breath in through your nose, then, without pausing, release the breath out through your mouth.
- Continue inhaling through your nose and exhaling out your mouth at a pace that is calm and steady for you, otherwise, inhale and exhale to a count of three seconds each.
- Notice as the air comes into your body and goes out.
- As you continue to inhale and exhale, notice the different sensations throughout your body and take note of any significant shifts in how you feel.

> *Take a deep breath, pick yourself up,*
> *dust yourself off, and start all over again.*
> —Frank Sinatra

EXERCISE 2: THE RELAXATION SIGH

Did you ever notice that your body will naturally cause you to sigh when you are under stress, sad, upset, or feeling overwhelmed?

This is because your body has a built-in system for stress relief; it's called the sigh. You may often sigh involuntarily, but you can use a sigh to release stress whenever you want. Below are breaths that can help you harness the power of the sigh. Notice that the breaths progress, building on the first very simple breath. Try each one and see which works best for you or do each breath, one after the other. Once you get comfortable with these breaths, you can create your own combination of breaths that makes you feel great.

Go to kerryfishercoaching.com for the video resource for this exercise.

PRACTICE

Level 1:
- Deeply inhale through your nose and exhale through your mouth.

Level 2:
- Inhale through your nose, then exhale through your mouth with a loud sigh.

Level 3:
- Inhale through your nose again, this time bringing your shoulders as far up as you can towards your ears.
- Hold for a moment.
- Exhale with an exaggerated and loud sigh while dropping your shoulders quickly.
- Notice how you feel (repeat if necessary).
- Feel free to go crazy here with the noises. Sound is a powerful way to release stress. This is a great way for you to release stress especially when you are feeling overwhelmed.

The Relaxation Sigh is a great tool to keep in your toolbox for those days where it feels like everything is falling apart. It is great to start your day this way, paying attention to your beautiful breath but this is also a great breath to take into your day. Anytime you begin to feel a bit overwhelmed or stressed, stop, and do these breaths.

Breathe.
Let go.
And remind yourself that this very moment is the
only one you know you have for sure.
—Oprah Winfrey

EXERCISE 3: BELLY BREATHING

Deep belly breathing, also known as diaphragmatic breathing, triggers a relaxation response in your body. This relaxation response is a result of the activation of the parasympathetic nervous system, known for its rest and digest function. Whereas the sympathetic system (commonly known for its fight or flight function) prepares the body for action or danger, the parasympathetic system (known as the rest and digest function) prepares the body for relaxation. When you breathe deep into your belly, the breath signals to your body that all is well. Our bodies are always listening to us. They pay close attention to our actions and respond to the signs we give. Remember, the breath and the body and brain are interconnected, constantly responding to one another and the world around us. All of this is to keep us safe. Truly, the body is an elegant and incredible masterpiece.

The following is an ideal relaxation breath practice. You can do this type of breath anytime you are feeling stressed or scatter-brained. It is also great for releasing anxiety.

PRACTICE

- Sit comfortably or lie comfortably on the floor .
- Notice how you're breathing right now? Are you breathing in your chest or deeper, into your belly? Simply notice how you typically breathe.
- Place both of your hands on your belly and breathe in through your nose, bringing the breath all the way down to your belly. Keep breathing in and filling your belly with air. Your hands should rise, like your belly is a beach ball.
- Breathe out slowly through your mouth.
- Repeat for three to five rounds of breath.
- Notice how you feel (repeat if necessary)

Discipline equals freedom.
—Jocko Willink

EXERCISE 4: BOX BREATHING

This is a great breath for keeping yourself calm, cool, and collected. This breath was developed by the U.S. Navy SEALs in order to maintain a sense of calm before dangerous missions. If it works for the SEALs, it can work for you too.

You will breathe in for a count of four, hold your breath for a count of four, breathe out for a count of four then hold your breath out for a count of four. Get it? 4-4-4-4 like the four sides of a box. Let's try it.

Go to kerryfishercoaching.com for the video resource for this exercise.

PRACTICE

- Sit comfortably or stand tall.
- Inhale through your nose to a count of four.
- Hold your breath for a count of four.
- Exhale through your nose to a count of four.
- Hold your breath for a count of four.
- Repeat for three to five rounds.
- Notice how you feel.

Virtually all of the oxygen we breathe is
used to produce energy in our cells.
—Dave Asprey

Box breathing is an incredible tool to help you stay calm and even keeled throughout the day. Start your day with box breathing but remember to use it anytime throughout the day when you need to tap into some peace and calm.

EXERCISE 5: ENERGIZING BREATH

It is absolutely crucial to have an assortment of relaxing breaths in your toolkit. Life presents many opportunities to use our tools of relaxation. However, there are also times when we need to increase our energy.

That is when a simple energizing breath can come in handy. This exercise is definitely on the more intense side and can be compared to a shot of espresso. It requires taking sharp inhales and quick exhales. It is very effective.

PRACTICE

- Bring your attention to your breath.
- Take three clearing deep breaths by deeply inhaling through your nose and exhaling through your mouth, pushing all the air out of your lungs.
- Take a sharp deep inhale through your nose, immediately followed by a forceful exhale out the mouth with a sound.
- Repeat this three to five times.
- Notice how you feel (repeat if necessary).

IMPORTANT NOTE

This energizing breath is much more intense than the other exercises above. You only need a few to feel the benefits. You may find the more you do, the more lightheaded you feel. Please be sure you are in a safe space when doing this exercise to eliminate falling.

We breathe so that the trees thrive
and the trees breathe so that we are able to live.
—Sanchita Pandey

HOW TO BRING BREATHING INTO YOUR DAY

Use these breathing techniques throughout your day whenever you need a quick pick me up, or you simply need a moment to relax. Any moment is a good moment to bring consciousness to your breath. A great way to incorporate this practice into your day seamlessly is to remember to do a breathing exercise right before each meal. Increase your relaxation by doing a brief breathing exercise after each meal as well. By adding a short practice before and after each meal, you will find that your days are calmer and easier. Give it a try.

A very important thing to remember is that these breaths are stress-relief tools. Each person is different, though, so try each exercise and see which one works for you and use the ones that feel good in your body. Learn what you need to learn, take what works and place the rest to the side for now. In the future, as your breath practice grows, you can come back to the other exercises and try them. Who knows, maybe one day these other exercises may resonate with you more.

Let's take a moment here for a quick side-note from me to you. All the answers are within you. You don't need to constantly look outside of yourself for ways to make your life better. You know what you need to do. This book is a gentle reminder of the things you already know. These are intuitive tools that many of us have lost touch with. They are the tools of gold that you can use to become the person you dream of being, the tools you need to live the life of your dreams.

REFLECT

1. Which relaxing breath exercise felt really good in your body?
2. Spend a few minutes thinking about, journaling, or recording your thoughts about:
   a. How you felt before each exercise.
   b. How you felt after each exercise.

    c.   Did any emotions come up for you? Accept all emotions that came up and do your best not to judge them. This is an observation of self, a look inward at what is going on within you.

3.   Reflect on those times in your day when you most need to relax and refresh. Resolve to use these techniques during those times.

4.   Make a list of times during your day that these exercises would be helpful.

5.   Consider setting an alarm a few times throughout the day to practice these techniques.

I was a competitive gymnast as a child, spending all my spare time in the gym. The gym was my haven, my second home. My coach, Diane Bitterman, was an incredible, forward-thinking coach, and she was always teaching us life lessons as we learned our sport.

One day, I was learning to do a backflip on the balance beam. The balance beam was my favorite event. I loved the challenge of trying to execute moves on the 4-inch beam. When you learn a new move, you first master it on the floor, then on a balance beam that sits on the floor. Then you move up to a beam about half of the real height with mats on either side and practice, practice, practice. Once you have mastered it, you go to the regulation size beam where your coach spots you and finally, you try it alone.

A backflip is scary on the balance beam. Launching yourself into the sky backwards and trying to land on the narrow beam is just as difficult as you would imagine it to be. I was nervous but felt confident. I did the move and as I went to land it, I realized I had miscalculated by a tiny bit, just enough for me to slide down along the side of the balance beam, scraping my thigh the entire way down and landing heavily on the mat with a thud. As I hit the mat, I noticed the pain in my thigh but within a moment, the pain fled from my mind as I realized I couldn't breathe at all. My breath had quite literally been knocked out of me.

As I lay there on the mat, incapable of breathing, I was scared. I kept trying to take a breath, but I couldn't take in any air. I wondered if I would ever be able to take another breath again.

That's when I saw my coach, Diane. She was hovering above me and then suddenly she bent down and knelt next to me. She caught my eye and said, "Kerry, you have to relax. Just relax your entire body and everything will be fine. You are fine. Just relax." As I looked into her reassuring eyes, I immediately relaxed and my body went limp. At that moment, there was a rush of air that flooded into my body. I could breathe once more!

As Diane helped me up, she gently said, "Kerry, remember, the best thing to do in any difficult situation is to relax. It can help you in every situation you find yourself in. When you stay relaxed, you can handle anything." It was great advice.

Dian gave me the opportunity to immediately practice this technique when she told me to get back up there on the beam and try it again. I gestured to my thigh which had a massive scrape all along the length of it. She smiled gently but firmly said it again, "You have to get back up there right now. Remember, stay relaxed." Yeah, easy for her to say!

I slowly got back up on the beam and began to breathe. I thought about how nice it was to simply have my breath. I relaxed my body. I quieted my mind and I executed the backflip, landing perfectly. I was thrilled, the lesson was instilled. I looked over at Diane, and she nodded, gestured for me to get down, and we tended to my wound. As she cleaned it, she said, "Remember what I taught you, Kerry. Stay relaxed, alert and relaxed. Then you are ready for anything."

I remember that advice any time I am scared, anytime I feel like I am in over my head, anytime my children are challenging me, anytime life is challenging me. I take a deep breath, remember that it is great to simply have the ability to breath, and I relax. And with that, I am able to take on the world!

Breathe deeply,
until sweet air extinguishes the burn of fear in your
lungs and every breath is a beautiful refusal
to become anything less than infinite.
—D. Antoinette Foy

*Meditation is like a gym
in which you develop
the powerful mental muscles
of calm and insight.*

—AJAHN BRAHM

CHAPTER 3

MEDITATION

MEDITATION AND THE BREATH

A meditation
Creates peace, promotes healing.
And there are many
—Dani G

*T*he old woman leaned in and said, "Meditate every single day for five minutes in the morning and five minutes in the evening. It will change your life." I'm not sure why but that was the event that started my daily meditation practice.

Before that, I had been meditating on and off ever since I was 20 years old. It never stuck. Yet once the old woman said this to me, meditation has been an everyday part of my life. It's interesting because I had always loved meditating but before that day, I would start meditating for a few months and eventually, I would stop. Something always got in the way, distracted me from what was a positive part of my life.

I guess it's true what they say: "When the student is ready, the teacher appears." That day, the old woman was my teacher. There was something so clear and knowing and wise in her eyes. I believed her. Or maybe, I was finally ready to listen. And maybe, just maybe, you are ready to listen as well. So, meditate every day, five minutes in the morning and then five minutes in the evening. It may just change your life.

If you do not have a meditation practice, this chapter is going to change your life. If you already have a meditation practice, begin to incorporate a short meditation at the start of your day to see if it changes the way you feel throughout the day. Beginning each day with meditation is a surefire way to add balance to your life.

Mediation has been practiced for thousands of years by spiritual seekers who sought to deepen their understanding of life. The practice of meditation has become more mainstream in recent years as an entire generation of overscheduled, overworked, overstressed people search for a way to balance their hectic lives. Meditation helps provide that balance by allowing you to slow down and tune in to this moment, to how you are feeling right now. It's powerful and life changing when you incorporate this simple practice into each one of your days.

Meditation doesn't cost anything, and it doesn't require any fancy equipment. You can do it anytime and anywhere. It's a tool that you can use whenever you need to feel more centered, calm, and relaxed. Daily meditation can reduce stress, anxiety, depression, and negative emotions while increasing focus, concentration, and memory. Adding meditation to your daily routine is one of the simplest ways to improve your emotional state and to bring a sense of ease and calm to your days.

Meditation allows you to get in tune with your body, mind, and spirit. It can increase your joy and decrease your stress. Meditation improves your focus, decreases brain fog, improves sleep, and reduces fatigue. Studies show that meditation can decrease anxiety and depression and lower your blood pressure. It can help you be more creative, more open, more patient, alert, and kinder.

The stress relief aspect of meditation is particularly fascinating. Let's see how that works by looking at the science. Don't worry, there will not be a test so just take in this information and marvel at the incredible genius of the human body. The nervous system is the part of your body that determines how you feel and prepares you for action. The nervous system is split into the central nervous system and the peripheral nervous system. The peripheral nervous system is further split into the somatic and the autonomic nervous system. The autonomic nervous system is the part of the nervous system we will be focusing on and that is split into the sympathetic and the parasympathetic nervous system.

The sympathetic nervous system prepares us for action. It is known as the "fight, flight, or freeze" aspect of the nervous system and it produces a chemical called cortisol whenever the body is under physical and emotional stress. Cortisol produces the "fight or flight" response in the body that is needed if we are confronted with a life-threatening situation. This is a good thing. But the problem comes in when our mind perceives a threat where there is none. Take traffic, for instance. If you are sitting in traffic and you begin to be upset, angry, or worried that you will be late for your appointment, your brain perceives this as a threat to you. And it responds the same way that it would respond to a true danger. In other words, your body will respond to the traffic the same way it would respond to being confronted by a lion, a tiger, or a bear. Oh my!

Yes, oh my, indeed! It's true, that's how it works. Our brain releases chemicals like cortisol to prepare to fight or flee. And while some cortisol is beneficial, too much cortisol causes damage to the body. It can disrupt your sleep, increase your blood pressure, and create feelings of anxiety. Here's the good news though. You CAN control this response; it isn't totally automatic!

So how do you control that response? Drum roll please...with meditation! Yes, meditation can signal to your body that everything is ok, that there is no need to fight or run. That you can relax. How does that work? Well, it has to do with the other part of the nervous system, the parasympathetic nervous system. The parasympathetic nervous system is known as the "rest and digest" aspect of the nervous system and it signals the body that all is safe and it is ok to relax. It is essential that we activate the parasympathetic nervous system in order to balance our hectic lives.

You might be wondering how on earth you are going to activate what appears to be an automatic bodily system. Well, this is where it gets super interesting. Bear with me for a tiny bit more science. The human nervous system is an automatic system; however, it can be influenced by our actions. The activities we choose to do, the situations we place ourselves in, and the people we surround ourselves with all contribute to whether we are activating the sympathetic, active part of our nervous system, or the parasympathetic or relaxing, resting part of our nervous system.

What this means is that we can choose activities that allow our body to rest and refresh. Activities like spending time in nature, listening to music, spending time with those you love, listening to music, or dancing can activate this relaxation response. Another thing that activates the parasympathetic nervous system is meditation. The best thing about meditation is that you can do it anywhere and at any time. Once you learn these simple meditation techniques, you can use them any time you begin to feel stressed.

MY MEDITATION PRACTICE BY DANI GLASSER

I have been meditating for so long that I don't even remember when I started. I do remember that I started with just being quiet and focusing on the breath. Inhaling and exhaling, doing my best to let my thoughts float by while focused breathing. It worked in that it kept me centered and grounded. I loved how I felt after doing it for just five minutes.

Originally, I used meditation to maintain stress. Today, I use it for healing, grounding, visualizing, motivation, inspiration, and more. It has gotten me through the most challenging times of my life.

Through the years, I have learned and discovered multiple forms of mediation. These days I prefer to use a combination of visualizations and energy work when I meditate. I also create meditations for myself and others, based on a word or intention. I use meditation to help find answers, connect within, heal myself, and conceptualize my life vision.

Whenever I find myself truly challenged, or in a space of discomfort, however, I do the one thing that always centers and calms me. No matter how upset I get, how stressed out my body feels, I always come back to the breath.

Let's go a little further and look closely at what type of meditation we are discussing here. There are so many types of meditations out there and there are also many myths around meditation. My intention is to examine these myths and to encourage you to think differently about meditation. It is commonly believed that meditation means that you clear your mind totally and that you revel in a calm, quiet mind. That your mind is just a clean, blank canvas there and we rest in the void. This is a great goal and is quite fabulous if you can get there but here's a little secret...that type of meditation is actually meant for practitioners who meditate hours every single day. People who are on a dedicated path towards enlightenment. Those practices are often practiced by monks who have given up everything and who quite literally sit in meditation for hours every day.

That is not to say that you need to give up everything to have that clear mind, that clean slate. You can achieve it if that is what you are aiming for but it is important to remember something. Most of us are living in the world. We are what is called a householder. We work, have families, friends, an active life filled with adult responsibilities. So perhaps the goal should be different. Perhaps the goal should be to tune into your mind instead of trying to clear your mind. Perhaps the goal should be to learn about yourself, to become intimately acquainted with who you really are. We do that by getting still and tuning in to all the thoughts that are going on in your mind. Not by clearing them out. See the difference?

Just like the heart beats involuntarily, the mind thinks involuntarily.
Thinking during meditation is actually an indication
that stress is leaving your body.
—Emily Fletcher

It is essential to recognize the fact that the brain is there to think, to create ideas and thoughts. So trying to stop the brain is a very difficult thing to do. However, allowing the brain to do what it does, which is think, while observing what you are thinking about, can be a true gamechanger. It can help you learn who you are and give you a glimpse into who you want to be.

Remember this, people on the path to meditation as a way to ultimate enlightenment often sit in meditation for hours each day, going deeper and deeper into the quiet. I don't know about you, but I don't have hours per day to meditate yet I still want to get the benefit of meditation. So how do we do that? We do that by readjusting our expectations.

So, what is a reasonable expectation? When you start meditating, your expectation should be simple. To begin, just have the intention that you will sit and meditate for the entire time frame you set aside, whether that is one snooze session, three minutes, 30 minutes or three hours. You begin where you are, and you work from there. There is a famous saying that the teacher should meet the student where they are and, in this case, since you are the teacher and the student, meet yourself where you are. Hit the snooze and try one of the practices below. Then do it again tomorrow and the next day; try it for a week. Then reassess.

If you can achieve total mind emptiness, great. If you can sit for the entire period until the alarm rings again, great. But if you can't, that's great too! Huh? That doesn't make sense to many of you, I know. Because we are taught that we have to do everything perfectly, and we need to do it "right," whatever that means. Begin by pushing aside any thoughts of what is right, what is perfect. Just let yourself rest in stillness and observe yourself for a few minutes. THAT is really the goal. The goal is self-observation, beginning to learn about yourself, and using that information you learn to transform yourself, to transform your life.

We don't meditate to get good at meditating.
We meditate to get good at life.
—Sharon Salzberg

Let's face it, we live in a world that is moving fast. We can barely keep up with it. Our modern world is a whirl of activity and motion. Taking just a few minutes to sit silently can do a world of good.

If you have ever observed a baby, you will notice that babies do lots of activity, then they slip into a period of rest. I remember that when my kids were babies, they would wake up from their naps and lay in their crib for a while, just looking around, cooing at themselves, checking out their hands and feet (and maybe putting them into their mouths) generally observing themselves and the world around them. They were simply relaxing. That is because in order to learn, they need to have down time to assimilate what they have learned.

The same is true for adults. We need down time, quiet time, to assimilate all that goes on in our crazy days. Which is why beginning your day with meditation is a fantastic practice to incorporate as you move towards your most extraordinary life.

Begin by reading through the meditation tips and then go over the various techniques. Look through the exercises and practice one. Then, set your alarm clock and begin your first morning snooze session meditation first thing tomorrow morning.

IVAN'S STORY: MY MEDITATION FRIEND

Did you know that I have a friend that helps me to meditate and enter a blissful state of high frequency, every time we get together?

This is a long-time friend that has been in my life for many years now, and I suspect this friendship will last many, many years. This being's beauty is incomparable and absolutely unique. Her wisdom is ancient and she has got the secrets of the Universe inside of her.

How was meditation introduced in our friendship? Let's just say that one day this friend kindly showed me how, by taking me into this inner journey and together we shared our energies, creating a strong bond and vibrating and similar frequencies.

My meditation friend is a tree. Every time I take a walk and pass by her, I approach her with respect, admiration and love. I gently touch her and we meditate for a short period of time. During this moment, time stops and reality expands into this All-Inclusive Love. There is a genuine feeling of Unity, Oneness, Ultimate Bliss.

Thank you, my dear friend.

~Ivan Garcia

BENEFITS OF MEDITATION

Daily Meditation Increases:

- focus
- concentration
- creativity
- patience
- alertness
- feelings of openness
- feelings of peace
- compassion
- gratitude
- Stress relief

Daily Meditation Decreases:

- anxiety
- depression
- lowers blood pressure
- anger
- negative emotions

Did you notice how meditation and breathwork have similar effects on the body? The reason for this is that both meditation and breathwork stimulate the relaxation response in the body. Pretty amazing, isn't it?

HOW TO MEDITATE

How do you get into a meditative posture (in other words, how to sit)? Do you need to sit cross legged on the ground when you meditate? Well, let me let you in on a little secret...it doesn't matter one bit. You see, you are meditating to make your life better, to make you better. So the most important thing is to be comfortable enough that you can sit throughout the meditation but not too comfortable that you fall asleep. Give yourself the greatest chance of success. Focus on getting into a comfortable seated position. It will be very difficult to maintain a meditative state if you aren't comfortable. However, you don't want to be too comfortable that you fall asleep. You are aiming to be comfortable enough to be able to sit for a few minutes while not being so comfortable that your meditation turns into an actual snooze. Remember, it's a Snooze Button Session, not a Snooze Session!

Meditation can be done in one of four postures: sitting, laying down, standing, and walking. Let's examine each one.

Sitting is the optimal position. It provides the perfect balance of focus and relaxation. When the body is upright, both the body and mind tend to be alert and attentive. At the same time, when we are seated, there is a certain degree of letting go and relaxation that naturally takes place. You can sit up in bed or sit on a chair, make the decision ahead of time where you will be meditating.

Lying down is another way to meditate. The catch here is that many people immediately feel a little bit too relaxed and drift off to sleep when they lay down. Since you will be doing this as soon as you awaken in the morning, after the alarm rings and you hit the snooze button, it might be difficult to stay awake while meditating in a lying down posture. Those moments when you first awaken are the moments when it is easiest to fall asleep. But give it a try and see how it works for you. if you notice that you fall back asleep, then sit upright instead.

Standing or **walking** are options as well. You won't fall asleep if you are standing (hopefully), but you may feel a bit too tense after just a few minutes of standing still in one place. It's worth a try though, just to experiment with which technique works best for you. Walking meditation is great if you are feeling especially tired. It is also good if you have an excess of energy or a very active mind. Walking and meditating will keep you concentrating deeply, and it will certainly calm down the thoughts that often come when you begin a meditation practice. You could stand up by a wall and see how that works.

PREPARE IN ADVANCE

Give yourself the best chance of success by deciding where you will be meditating. You can choose to sit up in bed and meditate there or you can create a separate meditation area. Get the area ready the night before or if possible, set up a permanent meditation area in your bedroom. Whatever you choose as your meditation seat, make sure you have everything ready to go so you can make the process as easy as possible in the morning when your alarm goes off.

If you are meditating on a cushion, have that set up in the corner of your room. If you are using a chair, that should be ready to go and set up close to your bed. Make it easy, make it painless, and you will have a much greater chance of success.

Tip: You may need to use the bathroom before your practices. In this case, hit the snooze, do what you need to do and then come back and wait for your alarm to go off again. Hit the snooze and meditate.

Remember: there is no right or wrong way. The main goal is simply to begin meditating. Don't worry so much about the details, just pick a method and try it. If it doesn't work well or you feel uncomfortable, then pick another method. Some Simple

POSTURE: SIT UP STRAIGHT!

Whichever method you choose, it is essential that you sit up straight, with your spine in alignment. Your shoulders are above your hips, your chin parallel to the ground. Make sure that your head is not jutting forward, it should be resting directly over your shoulders. An easy way to do this is to come to a comfortable seat and then straighten your spine. Imagine your shoulders over your hips. Envision each vertebrae stacking on top of the one below. Imagine a string on the top of your head, lifting you upward. As you sit up straight for meditation, begin to impress upon your brain that this upright posture is the one that you should use throughout the day. Keeping a straight spine while sitting or walking around is one of the easiest ways to bring a sense of strength and power into your daily life.

HAND POSITION

Rest your hands on your thighs or on your knees. You can even cradle one hand in the other and place them gently in your lap. If you want to get super fancy, you can place your hands in a mudra position. A mudra is a posture for your hand, and it is a very beautiful practice.

One of my favorite mudras is Gyana Mudra. Simply circle your thumb and index finger on each hand and have the middle, ring, and pinky fingers straight out. Another beautiful mudra is Buddhi Mudra. In this mudra you touch your thumb and pinky finger on each hand together and place them in a circle while the other fingers stand straight out. Finally, you can try Prana Mudra which is where you touch your thumb and your ring and pinky fingers together, creating a circle with the index and middle finger stretching straight. Once you have your mudra, place your hands on your knees or in your lap.

BODY POSITION

- Relax your forehead, corners of your eyes, corners of your mouth.
- Relax your jaw: part your lips, relax your tongue.
- Rest your gaze softly or close your eyes completely.
- Relax the corners of your mouth, gently part your lips.
- Keep your chin parallel with the ground.
- Straighten your spine.
- Allow your hips to feel heavy, rooted, grounded.
- Thighs, knees, shins, calves are relaxed.
- Feet and toes are relaxed.

Now that you have all the basics down, let's get to the meditations.

THE MEDITATIONS

EXERCISE 1: MEDITATION ON THE BREATH

This is an entry level meditation. Literally, anyone can do it. In fact, the main part of it is breathing, and you are already doing that, so you are halfway there before you even try. That's what makes it so simple. But don't confuse simple with easy. Although we are already breathing, we typically aren't concentrating on the breath and that is the main purpose of this exercise, to notice the breath and concentrate on the breath.

Meditation on the breath is a beautiful meditation because when we concentrate on the air coming in and out of the nose, it is very difficult to have a lot of thoughts running around in your mind. The breath is what sustains us, what gives us life and bringing your attention to your breath can allow you to tap into the beauty that is you and your amazing body. This can become a practice you take with you into your day. A moment of pausing, noticing the breath, and then feeling grateful for your breath.

Take a moment and think about how often you pay attention to your breath each day. Sure, you might notice it when you are exerting yourself and gasping for breath or perhaps you might notice when you get really stressed out where it is a bit difficult to breathe. Maybe you notice your breath when you aren't feeling well, and you are struggling to breath. But what about all the rest of the time? Are you paying attention to your breath at all? Most likely, the answer is no. So today, we begin our love affair with our breath. By meditating on the breath.

Are you ready? Let's try it. Yes, let's jump right in. You already have the first part down, the breathing, so let's focus on the second part, the PAYING ATTENTION to the breath.

Meditation is to be aware of every thought and of every feeling,
never to say it is right or wrong but just to watch it and move with it.
In that watching, you begin to understand
the whole movement of thought and feeling.
And out of this awareness comes silence.
—Jiddu Krishnamurti

EXERCISE 2: THE CLEANSING BREATH

- Take a deep breath in through your nose.
- Exhale through your mouth.
- That's the cleansing breath.
- Take two more cleansing breaths, in through the mouth and out through the nose.

Ok, did you do it? If not, then take a moment now to simply go ahead and do it right now. As you are reading this, practice and learn. This way, when the alarm goes off tomorrow, you will be ready.

Cleansing Breath Plus Focus on the Breath Meditation

- Once you have your three cleansing breaths down, try it with your eyes closed. Take three cleansing breaths.
- Now, close your mouth and breathe in and out through your nose, noticing the breath as it comes in and out. Continue to breathe in and out through your nose.
- Focus your attention on the tip of your nose, right at your nostrils and feel the cool breath coming in through your nose on the inhale and then the warm breath moving out on the exhale.
- Inhale the cool air into your nose, exhale the warm air out of your nose.

Practice

Now that you know the technique, set a timer for three minutes, close your eyes. Take your three cleansing breaths and begin to pay attention to the breath. Focus on the air coming in and out. If your mind wanders, gently bring your attention back to the breath. When the timer goes off, take three cleansing breaths to complete the meditation.

There. You did it. That's meditation. Woo-hoo! I know what you're thinking...What? It must be more complicated than that. Well. It can be, but that's the cool thing about meditation, it doesn't have to be. It can be simple and eventually, it will even get easy. You are just meditating on the breath, simply placing all your focus on paying your breath.

REFLECT

Think about what happened as you were paying attention to your breath. Did you notice your mind wandering? If so, that's ok. Part of meditation is tuning into what is going on in your mind. So just notice that your mind has wandered and bring it back to your breath, to your meditation.

> *If you meditate regularly, even when you don't feel*
> *like it, you will make great gains, for it will allow you to see*
> *how your thoughts impose limits on you. Your resistances*
> *to meditation are your mental prisons in miniature.*
> —Ram Dass

EXERCISE 3: MANTRA MEDITATION

This is a very simple meditation. I like to think of it as an entry level meditation for people who want to try meditation but don't know where to start. It is also extremely powerful for people who have been meditating for years. This is the type of meditation used in Transcendental Meditation; however, you don't have to be a Transcendental Meditation practitioner to try this.

The first step is to pick your mantra. The word mantra might seem intimidating to you but don't let it. Mantra simply means a word or phrase, sometimes thought of as a sacred formula. We use our mantra by repeating it over and over in order to enhance and focus concentration during meditation.

How do you pick your mantra? This is the fun part. You pick a mantra that you feel comfortable with.

As a yoga teacher, I began my mantra meditation by using the word Om. The word Om is defined by the Merriam-Webster dictionary as "a mantra consisting of the sound \'ōm\ and used in contemplation of ultimate reality," as well as "order of merit." Om is the universe, the past, the present, and the future, all that was, all that is, all that will be is om. You can also use a two-word phrase as a mantra like "I am" or "just this."

Mantras

- Om
- Just this: Breathe in *just*, Breathe out *this*.
- Peace/Love: Breathe in *peace*, breathe out .
- Peace/calm: Breathe in *peace*, breath out *calm*.
- I am: Breathe in *I*, breathe out *am*.
- Create your own mantra.

Practice: Mantra Meditation

- Close your eyes and relax your forehead; relax the corners of your mouth.
- Relax your shoulders away from your ears.
- Now take three cleansing breaths. Breathe in through your nose, open your mouth and exhale out through your mouth.
- Breathe in and then as you breathe out, think of your mantra or seed word.
- If you are using a two-word phrase, breathe in and think one word and breathe out and think the second. For example, if your mantra is "just this," you would breathe in and think, "just" and breathe out and think "this."

Quiet the mind, and the soul will speak.
—Ma Jaya Sati Bhagavati

EXERCISE 4: NOTICE THE THOUGHTS MEDITATION

The Notice the Thoughts Meditation is a great meditation regardless of how much experience you have with meditation. If you are new to meditation, this is a very good entry into the world of meditation and the benefits of meditation. One word of warning though. When you first begin to slow down and tune into your mind, you might be surprised by what you find.

PRACTICE

- Sit in a comfortable seat and take three cleansing breaths (see above).
- Relax the top of your head, your forehead, the corners of your eyes, the corners of your mouth. Relax your shoulders, your arms, your hands and fingers. Relax your torso, your thighs, your feet and toes.
- Take three more cleansing breaths.
- Begin to focus all of your attention on your mind.
- What are you thinking about?
- Allow the thoughts to flow in but don't try to control them.
- As the thoughts flow into your brain, observe them, and then let them go.
- Imagine your thoughts are like clouds in the sky. The clouds drift across and then they float away, just like your thoughts do. In and then out.
- Remember not to judge the thoughts; just notice them.
- Follow the thoughts as they go by.
- Notice, do you have the same thoughts over and over? Or perhaps one thought goes by and then it drags you into a rabbit hole, thinking about that one thing. Notice, observe, relax, breathe.
- When the alarm goes off again, you can get up and start your day or you can choose to press the alarm one more time and observe your thoughts for one more Snooze Button Session.

OBSERVE THE THOUGHTS

I remember the first time I took a yoga class when I was 21 years old. I was backpacking at the time, traveling the world to find myself by purposely losing myself. I was living and working on a kibbutz, and I heard about a yoga class they were offering. I didn't even know what yoga was nor had I ever heard of it but the teacher was hot, so I decided to go to the class. Hey, what do you expect from a 21-year-old?

I loved the vibe from the moment I entered the room. Wooden floors, buddha statues all around, the sweet sense of incense in the air, yoga mats laid out in straight rows. Plus, a hot yoga teacher in short shorts at the front of the class. Oh yes, I was home.

I went to stand on one of the mats, right up at the front of the class in front of the teacher. I was ready to wow him to be honest. The teacher put on some music and began the class. I really enjoyed the flow and as a former gymnast, the physical practice came very easy to me. I looked like I had been doing yoga for years. What did not come easy to me was facing what was happening in my mind. It was a chaotic mess in there.

You see, when I stood on the yoga mat and began to match my breath to movement as the teacher started speaking softly and with an encouraging tone and the music began to work its magic, it evoked emotions I didn't even know I had. I noticed that my mind could not relax. As I began to pay attention to what was happening in my mind, perhaps for the first time in my entire life, I realized that I had this endless stream of thinking going on. Endless.

Even worse, I was horrified to realize that the stream was not nice. It felt like my mother was in there reprimanding me and telling me all the things I was doing wrong or could do better. My attention was skipping around from the hot teacher to the lady in front of me whose underwear was showing to the fact that my leg really hurt when I put it in that position and then back to the hot teacher. It was endless. Frenetic and endless.

After class that day, I went up to the teacher and told him that I had a real problem, that my mind was completely and utterly unruly. That maybe, just maybe, I was crazy. The teacher just laughed and patted me on the shoulder. He said, "Oh, don't worry, we all have that. We call it the monkey mind." He smiled and told me to come back again the next day and then with one last reassuring pat, he walked away.

As I walked out, I realized that if any person I knew spoke to me the same way that my mind was talking to me, I would immediately eliminate them from my life. I resolved, in that moment, to learn everything I needed to learn to tame that wild monkey mind of mine. To learn all the techniques, the tips, the tricks, to become calmer and kinder. And that, my friends, was the beginning of my love affair with yoga, meditation, breathwork, and mindfulness practices. I am happy to report that more than 30 years later, my monkey mind is tamed, although, I must admit, it takes constant practice and attention to keep it in line!

EXERCISE 5: 4-MINUTE MEDITATION

There are no ordinary moments.
—Dan Millman

This meditation is from one of the foremost spiritual teachers of our day, Dan Millman. I read Dan Millman's book, *The Way of the Peaceful Warrior* when I was a teenager, and it simply transformed my life. That book rocked me to my very core, spoke to me on the deepest level. Fast forward 30 years, and I had the thrill of a lifetime when I met Dan Millman at a workshop. I got to spend the entire weekend learning from him in person. He was every bit as amazing as his book was. At that workshop, he taught us this -minute meditation, and it became an everyday part of my life.

This is my favorite go-to meditation when I am pressed for time. I try to do it at least once a day. Originally, I would only do it in the morning or at night but eventually, I realized that I could do this meditation anywhere. So I might do it while I am on the subway, waiting for a plane, sitting and waiting for one of my kids. I use it all the time.

You can go to Dan Millman's website to get the audio version of this meditation, and I highly suggest you do so. Just hearing his voice guiding you can take you into another world.

To do the meditation, Dan uses a very easy to remember format. Remember the word **TORA** then **6 S words.**

i.   TORA stands for *thoughts, objects, relationships, actions.*

ii.   6 S words are: *sensations, smell, sight, sound, self, savor (taste).*

iii.   You start out with three cleansing breaths (those are always helpful).

iv.   Then you take a nice inhale and, on the exhale, release all thoughts.

v.   Next, inhale and on the exhale, release all objects; you no longer have any possessions, let them go.

vi.   Inhale, exhale, and release relationships. This one can be tough.

vii.   Inhale, exhale, and release all actions, nothing left to do.

viii.   Inhale, exhale, release all sensations, nothing left to feel.

ix.   Inhale, exhale, release all sense of taste.

x.   Inhale, exhale, release all sense of smell.

xi.   Inhale, exhale, release all sense of sight.

xii.   Inhale, exhale, release all sense of sound.

xiii.   Inhale, exhale, release all sense of self.

xiv.   Breathe here in this space, inhaling and exhaling slowly and easily.

xv.   When you are ready, finish with three cleansing breaths.

xvi.   Let yourself return into your body. You might feel a strong sensation like you are being heavily dropped into your body.

xvii.   Sit for a few moments and savor the feeling that you have all the things you have, a body, senses, relationships, possessions.

Note: If you want to find other simple ways to create ease and flow in your life, check out Dan Millman's website and his prolific writings. I consider him my lifelong, foundational teacher, and I have followed his work for over 30 years. Sometimes you meet someone you admire and

Tools for Extraordinary Living

they don't live up to his expectations but when I spent time with Dan Millman, he not only met my expectations, he exceeded them greatly.

ONE LIGHT, MANY LAMPS

In 2019, I saw that Dan Millman was going to be doing a weekend workshop just a few short hours away from my house. I made an instant decision to go and finally meet my lifelong teacher in person. I was absolutely ecstatic.

I got there early and had a chance to say hello to Dan before the workshop started. I also put my stuff on a chair in the first row so that my view of my hero would be unobstructed. When I met him, he was as down to earth as I had envisioned him to be. Although he is one of the pioneers in the personal growth arena, he is humble and kind. He is everything a spiritual teacher should be.

During the weekend, Dan set aside hours so we could come to sit with him and speak to him privately. Again, I got there early, so I would have time with him. I had brought my favorite book, The Way of the Peaceful Warrior *with me for him to sign. It was the book that introduced Dan to me all those years ago when I was a starry eyed college student.*

I sat down and began to chatter away. After a few moments, I relaxed and realized I wanted HIM to speak. I asked him what his views were of gurus. He told me he didn't believe in gurus. I mentioned that my favorite quote was, "When the student is ready, the teacher will come." As I looked at him, I was sure he was the teacher for me. I decided to be bold and asked him if he had ever considered creating a small group of students he could mentor personally. I knew he lived close to me, so I would be first in line.

He looked at me quietly for a moment and then he said that no, he didn't think he would ever do that. He didn't believe in guruship he repeated. Then he said this: "I believe there is one light, many lamps." I understood what he meant; there would not be any private tutoring for me.

I jokingly said to him, "Damn, when WILL my teacher appear?" To which he responded, "The teacher is within."

I knew that was a mike drop moment plus there was a line of students waiting to speak with him, so I gently said thank you and then I got up, gave him an hug, and walked away. I remember thinking that I had just met a true teacher. A teacher who understood that the best teachers allow the students to find the way themselves.

> *The mediocre teacher tells.*
> *The good teacher explains.*
> *The superior teacher demonstrates.*
> *The great teacher inspires.*
> —William Arthur Ward

EXERCISE 6: 6 PHASE MEDITATION

The 6 Phase Meditation by Vishen Lakhiani is a true gamechanger. It changed my life, it changed my husband's life, and it can change your life too. Vishen Lakhiani is one of the most amazing spiritual teachers I have come across. He has created a platform called Mindvalley where there are courses, called quests, that you can take to upgrade your mind, body, and spirit. Mindvalley has been a game changer for me, providing the information and teachings I needed in a format that I could easily fit into my life.

The 6 Phase Meditation was created by Vishen Lakhiani as a way to create the life of your dreams. Vishen studied meditation since he was a teenager and, as an adult, he studied with all the top meditation teachers in the world. He took all of the best practices from the different meditation techniques and put it all together to create the 6 Phase Meditation. Here it is, used with permission from Vishen Lakhiani. You can google the 6 Phase Meditation and follow along with Vishen; he is a master meditation teacher.

PRACTICE

- Relaxation
  - o Sit up straight, inhale deeply, and exhale to close your eyes.

o   Relax your forehead, the corners of your eyes, the corners of your mouth.

o   Relax your shoulders, arms, hands and fingers.

o   Relax your chest, back, belly, hips, legs, feet and toes.

o   Inhale deeply and exhale slowly.

- **Phase 1**: Compassion for Self and Others
    o   Think of someone you truly love.
    o   Feel compassion in your heart.
    o   Give the emotion a color.
    o   Feel the color surrounding you like a light.
    o   Take a deep breath and expand.
    o   Expand the light to envelop you, expand outwards to fill the room and then the building you are in.
    o   Expand the light even further to fill your town, your city, your country with the light of love, compassion.
    o   Allow the light to encompass all human beings, plants, animals and to expand across planet earth.
    o   See planet earth covered in the light of love.

- **Phase 2**: Gratitude: Expand Your Levels of Happiness
    o   Think of three things you are grateful for that happened in the past day, week, or month. Feel the emotion and feel the gratitude.
    o   Feel the emotion associated with each thing whether it is a gift, a person, a kind word.
    o   Think of three things you are grateful for at work. It could be a coworker, a project you are working on, the pay you receive, the atmosphere at work. Feel the emotion and give thanks.
    o   Think of three aspects of your being whether it is your body, your mind, or your soul, a character trait, an act or a personal quality you embody. Give thanks. Feel joy and positive emotions as you think of this aspect of yourself.

- **Phase 3**: Forgiveness
  - o Think of something negative that has happened. It can be big or small.
  - o Bring the person or situation to your mind and truly feel the feelings you have experienced. Feel pain, feel anger.
  - o Take three relaxation breaths.
  - o Now think about the situation from the other person's point of view.
  - o Remember that hurt; people hurt people.
  - o Now, think about how it made you feel, how it helped you, how it made you understand.
  - o Forgive them, let it go.
  - o If the charge associated with the situation is done, then you are finished.
  - o If not finished, revisit this again tomorrow.
  - o Repeat until all feelings associated with the situation or person have no charge associated with it.

- **Phase 4**: Envisioning Your Future
  - o Think about what you want in the future.
  - o Create a vision for your life three years ahead.
  - o We tend to overestimate what we can do in one year but underestimate what we can do in three years, so choose big goals.
  - o Think about what you want in your career, love, health, adventure.
  - o Expand your body, mind, soul, and being in all ways.
  - o Feel and see the picture as vividly as possible. What do you see, hear, smell, feel?
  - o Think of your goals unfolding and now imagine all your goals have been accomplished.
  - o How does it feel to have this goal accomplished?
  - o Linger with future visions. Use all your senses.
  - o As if you have this goal accomplished.
  - o Focus on feelings.

- **Phase 5**: Plan Your Perfect Day
  - o Now imagine your perfect day.
  - o Imagine what you will do when you first wake up.
  - o Imagine your morning. What will you do? Will you work? Exercise? Spend time with family?
  - o Construct your perfect morning. Everything is going perfectly, all is well.
  - o Then what? What do you do for the late morning, early afternoon? Imagine you are productive, on target, on track, all is going as planned. Meetings are going the way you dream of, your work is getting done, you are interacting well with everyone you meet.
  - o Now imagine your lunch. It is the perfect lunch. Who will you eat with? What will you eat? Treat yourself well, make it the best lunch you can imagine.
  - o Think about the afternoon now. What will you be doing, what activities, work will you do? Who will you spend time with?
  - o Now it is dinner time. Who do you eat with? What do you eat? Imagine it perfectly, down to the smallest detail.
  - o Imagine the end of your day, your evening. Will you relax, spend time with family or friends?
  - o Now imagine you are back in your bed; you are reflecting back upon your perfect day, and you resolve to have another perfect day tomorrow.
  - o You go to sleep and have a very restful, relaxing, refreshing sleep.

- **Phase 6**: Blessing
  - o Think of a person you really like. Imagine them in front of you.
  - o Ask them for a blessing, to bless you and allow you to be safe and protected.
  - o Take a deep breath in and a long breath out, Repeat this two more times. Blink your eyes open.
  - o Have a great day

Note: To learn more about the 6 Phase Meditation, you check out Minevalley.com for more information or go to YouTube and search for the 6 Phase Meditation. You can also buy his latest book where he discusses the method in detail.

Go to kerryfishercoaching.com for the video resource for this exercise.

Most human beings underestimate
just how powerful their thoughts are in
creating the world around them.
—Vishen Lakhiani

EXERCISE 7: GUIDED MEDITATION

A guided meditation is a lovely way to learn to meditate. This guided meditation will help you to focus on creating the best life you can possibly live.

Go to kerryfishercoaching.com for the video resource for this exercise.

How to Bring Meditation into Your Day

The meditations above are there to help get you started. If this is the first time you have meditated then simply begin with the Breath Meditation or the Notice the Thoughts Meditation. There are also some great guided meditations you can do during your Snooze Button Sessions on the website Simple Tools for Extraordinary Living. Find links in the resources tab. If you already have a meditation practice, then take it up a level and add meditation into your morning routine every day. Beginning your day with meditation is a great way to bring a sense of ease and balance into your life.

Once you have established your morning meditation practice, you can bring meditation into your day. Anytime that you are feeling stressed, stop and focus on your breath or on your thoughts. You can also record your own meditation and listen to that whenever you need a quick break. Bringing meditation into your life will change everything in your life.

Take a moment right now and do this exercise with me. Think about a typical day for you. Think about the moment the alarm clock goes off. What do you typically do? Hit the snooze and doze off again? Then what happens? Do you wait until you simply have no more time and then jump up and race around to get everything done? Now, go through your day and think about all the things that you did from when you woke up until you finally collapsed in your bed at night. Think about all those activities, work, running around and achieving that you did. Just thinking about it can exhaust you. And guess what, those activities do exhaust you because they are exhausting.

Now think about this. What if, instead of just going through your day on autopilot, trying to get to the end of the night where you can drop into bed, what if you took a few minutes when you begin your day and then a few more breaks throughout the day to stop, sit silently. Yes, I'm saying it. What if you sat there and MEDITATED a few times a day?

So here's a little challenge. Start each day by hitting your snooze button and sitting up nice and straight and meditating until the alarm clock goes off again. And then get up and go through your day. Noticing that you feel calmer, more centered, more focused is great. That's information for you that it's working. So then, find another few minutes in the day, perhaps before bed, to again sit silently and concentrate on your breath. And see what happens. Keep adding these short bursts of meditation throughout your day and simply observe how you feel.

Check out my online meditation course if you would like to go deeper into your meditation practice.

Many students of yoga perform their exercise
in a haphazard way; then wonder why they do not 'get
anywhere' and why they fail to feel communion with the
Infinite even after apparently serious meditation.
—Paramahansa Yogananda

Reflect

1. Reflect on how you feel before you meditate and how you feel after you meditate.
2. Record your reflections by journaling as soon as you are done meditating.
3. Reflect on which meditation practice felt the best in your body.
4. Reflect on those times in your day when you most need to meditate. Remember to use these techniques during those times.
5. Make a list of times during your day that these exercises would be helpful.
6. Consider setting an alarm a few times throughout the day to practice these techniques.
7. Begin a practice of journaling after each meditation session.

QUIET THE MIND AND THE SOUL WILL SPEAK

I began a daily, regular meditation practice when I did my yoga teacher training. At the time, I was practicing law, and I had promised myself that if I threw myself into yoga and meditation and practiced every day, that I would become a full time wellness educator. I was very disciplined and focused.

As I began to meditate daily, I noticed that my mind was a chaotic mess. It would jump from here to there and back again. Even worse, my mind seemed to circle around to the same thoughts.

I learned a lot about myself during this time period. I learned that I had a lot of emotions that I typically ignore. I learned that I had a lot of fear. I learned that I didn't love myself. I learned that I typically focused on what was going wrong in my life, not what was going right. I learned all these things and more. Some of the things I learned were a total shock to me and some were things I knew but didn't think about consciously.

As the time passed, it felt like a virtual volcano of emotions and thoughts. To be honest, it was what I call a dark moment of the soul for me. A moment where I faced the absolute and ultimate truth about myself. It was tough as

I became conscious of all of the things that I usually simply shoved down; things I usually just ignored.

As these emotions and thoughts rose to the surface, I briefly thought about running away. I briefly thought about abandoning this new, bold, brave path.

One day, during a particularly deep meditation, I had an epiphany. I understand that I always have this stream of thoughts running through my head, and it is my brain and my body speaking to me. At that moment, I realized that I wanted to bring all of these unconscious thoughts into my consciousness, to hear the thoughts, learn from the thoughts I have that are clamoring for my attention and then morph and change, transform and grow into the next grandest version of myself.

That decision to focus on what my mind was telling me changed everything. As a matter of fact, it is the reason that you are reading this book today.

This, my friends, is how powerful it is to quiet your mind and allow yourself to learn more about who you are. You give yourself the chance to heal your wounds, to morph and grow, transform and change. To become the very best version of yourself you can possibly be.

Come, take my hand. Let's add meditation into your daily practices.

Between stimulus and response there is a space.
In that space is our power to choose our response.
In our response lies our growth and our freedom.
—Viktor Frankl

Movement is a medicine
for creating change in
a person's physical, emotional,
and mental states.

—CAROL WELCH

CHAPTER 4

MOVEMENT: EXERCISE, DANCE, YOGA, STRETCHING

Life is like riding a bicycle.
To keep your balance, you must keep moving.
—Albert Einstein

*I*t was 2019, and I was hiking Mt. Washington with my five children, my oldest son's girlfriend, and my husband. From the very beginning of the hike, I felt dizzy and disoriented. I was also feeling like my brain was fuzzy and not working properly. I was carrying a very heavy pack which I wasn't used to, and it was getting hot with the sun beating down upon me. I knew early on that I was in trouble but something kept me from turning back. I knew that if I turned back that my youngest kids, who were 11 and 13 at the time, would want to continue on even if I stopped. The steepness of the hike and the danger inherent in such a hike made the idea of stopping one I wouldn't even consider.

At a certain point in the hike, my husband sat down and said he wasn't going any further. My youngest kids turned to me and begged me to keep going. I knew I shouldn't but as I looked at their faces, I just couldn't say no. So I ignored all the screaming my body was doing and continued on.

We were at the very last stretch, and we had to descend into a valley before hiking up the last, very steep uphill to our final destination. As I walked down into the valley, my heart was pounding in my ears. My cheeks flushed; my temples were pounding. I knew I was in trouble. But instead of stopping, I continued on.

When we got to the bottom of the valley, the kids found a snow patch to play in. As they frolicked in the snow, I contemplated the final uphill stretch. It seemed impossible to me. I gazed past the final stretch at Mount Rainier which soared majestically behind Mount Washington. It was beautiful, unknowable, mysterious. I barely cared. I was just focused on getting to the top and then somehow, getting the hell off this mountain.

We began the final climb and my kids, all in their teens and early twenties, kept a very quick pace. They climbed and climbed, and I struggled to keep up. My heart felt like it might explode. It was pounding in my ears. Messaging me to stop, stop, stop. I ignored it, eyes on the top of the climb.

When we got to the top of the climb, I was even dizzier and more disoriented. I couldn't think. I sat down, ate two bananas, some granola bars, and drank all of my water. I thought I was going to die. My kids ran around the clearing, oblivious to the danger I was in.

Soon enough it was time to go back. We had to descend back into the valley and then up the hill to where my husband was sitting. Then beyond that, there was the whole rest of the hike downwards. The daunting thing was this valley-mountain pass right ahead of us though. It was steep. My older kids went ahead while I stayed back with my two youngest. They were struggling, I was struggling. I kept looking up the mountain, wondering how the hell I would be able to get my kids and myself back there. I wasn't sure I could. Physically I was in terrible shape. I honestly thought I might die on that mountain. I almost didn't care if I did. The mountain was spinning around me, my head was aching and no matter what I did, I couldn't catch my breath.

At this moment, my daughter turned to me and said she couldn't make it. As I heard her say this, a wave of adrenaline hit me. I told her not to worry, she would make it, we would just go slow. Step after painstaking step, we climbed. I focused only on making sure my children got to the top, back to where my husband was sitting. Then I could drop dead, I thought.

We finally got to the top of the mountain, and I sat down heavily, trying to catch my breath. I was so winded. I looked out over Mount Rainier. It was majestic, but I still didn't care. I just wanted to get the hell off that mountain.

The trip back down was arduous, but I was motivated to just get back to the car. Again, I kept my eye on the goal and ignored my body. We made it to the car, and I finally allowed myself to feel what I really felt. I was in trouble, I knew it. The next few days were a blur. My mind was unfocused, confused. I was hallucinating; I was sick. I went to the hospital twice and they gave me fluids.

When I finally was able to fly home, I went to my own doctor and after a ton of testing, he found that I was in bad shape, all my numbers were off, I was not ok. The following months I had to see a neurologist bi-weekly, and I worked hard to get my health back. It was a tough journey back for me, and I feared that my brain would never get back to normal. Luckily, it did.

Once I was totally better, I decided I needed to focus on my fitness. I am blessed to be naturally thin, but I now knew that thin didn't mean in shape. So I focused on muscle building, cardio. I studied courses in health and fitness. I dedicated myself to getting into the best shape of my life. I did this by first adding movement to my day, first thing when I woke up, during my Snooze Button Session. Beginning my day with movement put that idea into my head that I should move all day long. And I have added movement to all parts of my day. And you can too. It all begins with your morning Snooze Button Session.

Movement is absolutely essential to your well-being. Humans are designed for motion. We are meant to walk, run, jump, skip, hop, dance, sprint, squat, twist, turn, and bend. Movement is necessary if you want to have a healthy body and without movement, our bodies begin to deteriorate. In order to have physical strength, a muscular and toned physique, good cardiovascular and circulatory health, we must move.

Modern society does not support a lifestyle of movement. With the advent of office jobs and most recently, the massive explosion of technology, many of us spend a lot of time sitting. We have become a sedentary society. These days, it is common to sit for 12 hours a day or more. Take a moment right now to think about how many hours per day you sit. Think about how many hours you are sitting in front of your computer, commuting in your car, sitting down to meals, watching television. It may surprise you to add up the number of hours each day that you sit.

In early human civilization, people moved from place to place in order to secure adequate food and shelter for the group. Early Neanderthals lived a relatively nomadic lifestyle, hunting and gathering throughout a region and as they circulated through several temporary camps. Other groups had one central camp from which they radiated outwards in their search for good hunting grounds. Whether hunting or gathering, early man walked miles each day in order to survive. Their lifestyle provided them with all the movement and exercise they needed to be strong and healthy. As humans shifted to an agrarian society, they remained active tending to their fields and livestock, and they spent most of their time in an active mode, sitting only three to four hours per day.

In modern times, we no longer need to hunt and gather. We no longer need to search for shelter. Most of us are not tending to our fields. This has led many people to lead sedentary lives. Hunched over computers and cellphones, modern man is moving less and less with each passing year. This has been exacerbated in recent years as the world has shifted to virtual work. We are sitting more than ever before and this is having a huge negative impact on our health. In Western societies, it is estimated that the average person sits for 10-12 hours per day.

Excessive sitting leads to many diseases and conditions like obesity, cardiovascular disease, depression, back pain, and hypertension.

Remember, our bodies are built for action, built for movement. When we stop moving and start sitting more, our physical bodies pay the price. When our physical body begins to deteriorate, it affects our emotions and our minds. Remember, we are one whole. Our body affects our mind, and our mind affects our body. It works as one cohesive system.

Exercise and movement can have a beneficial effect on the actual structure of the brain. A recent study by Simone Kuhn from the Max Planck Institute for Human Development revealed evidence that regular outdoor walks improve brain structure and mood. The scientists noted that there were changes to the prefrontal cortex which improved concentration and working memory. The evidence showed that movement improves neural connections in the brain. Neural connections are the way the nervous system communicates with muscle cells, nerve cells, and gland cells. The brain has the ability to shape and reshape itself by creating these neural connections. Adding movement into your life helps to build stronger connections and to quite develop different areas of the brain. This provides a variety of benefits.

A lot of evidence indicates that moderate exercise a few times a week improves thinking skills, brain health, and cognitive functioning. According to a study done by James Blumenthal, "Our operating model was that by improving cardiovascular risk, you're also improving neurocognitive functioning." The study, published in the journal *Neurology*, showed that when you add exercise to your life, "You're improving brain health at the same time as improving heart health." It is becoming increasingly clear that regular physical activity plays a very important role in maintaining a healthy body and mind at every age.

Movement also helps strengthen your muscles which is very important, especially as you get older. Sarcopenia, or muscle loss, is a common occurrence in people as they age and muscle loss leads to balance issues which may cause falls. Preventing this is as easy as getting regular exercise in order to keep your muscles strong and healthy so that you can maintain your stability, balance, and coordination. Movement also helps you to maintain bone density. Exercises like weight training and weight bearing exercises like jogging and walking help to build bone mass which is essential to healthy aging.

CHASE'S CLIMBING COMMITMENT

My youngest son Chase was always a very active child. He was born to run and move and climb. Our family had been members of a local indoor climbing gym for a few years but the global pandemic put a stop to that for a long time. We finally decided to go back and when we did, I noticed that Chase was getting really good, really fast. We like to boulder which means climbing without a harness, relying on your own ability to stay on the wall.

The difference in our climbing style was apparent from the start. Whereas I clung to the wall, fearfully looking down to see how far I would fall, Chase had no fear. He scaled the wall quickly and easily, as if he were a monkey. In bouldering, they rate the climbs on a scale ranging from V0 to V17 but our gym only goes up to V11 which is basically like trying to climb a flat wall with tiny protuberances. We both started at V0 but within a few weeks Chase was already climbing V3s while I was still climbing V1s and trying to climb V2s with little success.

Chase loved it so much that he decided to join the climbing team and that was when I saw a massive improvement in his skills. Before long, he was easily climbing V4s and then V5s. Eventually, he even mastered a V6 which was amazing to see. Chase was consumed with going to the gym and one day, he declared, "I'm going to go to the gym every day for 100 days." I smiled and nodded, "Yeah, sure, me too." I never thought he was serious. Well, I was wrong! Every day, Chase asked to go to the gym. 30 days, 60 days. He was getting closer and closer.

One day he was really tired and felt a little bit sick, he had a lot of homework and he said his muscles were sore. I suggested that he stay home to rest. He looked at me like I was crazy. His exact words were, "Mom, when you make a commitment to do something like this, you stick with it. No excuses. Excuses make you weak. I am strong." He went that day and every day until he hit 100 days. At that point, I figured we could get a break. I was starting to think we lived at the climbing gym. But no, when Chase hit 100 days, it just motivated him to keep going. Imagine commitment like that. So if he can do it, we can do it too.

As a side note, I know you're curious, yes, I accompanied him on most of those days at the gym. And yes, I am still climbing V2s. But, I am able to actually climb most of them now, and I am beginning to work on V3s. That's progress!

If that story doesn't motivate you to move, then maybe this will. Check out some of the benefits of movement.

BENEFITS OF MOVEMENT

Movement Improves:
- flexibility
- range of motion
- feelings of well being
- balance
- energy
- alertness
- endurance
- heart health
- mental clarity
- feelings of calmness
- bone strength

Movement Reduces:
- stress
- depression
- anxiety
- high blood pressure
- risk of stroke
- muscle tightness

THE EXERCISES

EXERCISE 1: DYNAMIC STRETCHES: STANDING ROUTINE

Stretching in the morning is a great way to start your day. You may notice that when you first wake up, your body feels stiff and inflexible. This is because as you sleep, the fluid in your joints, called synovial fluid, leaches out of the joint space and into the bones that make up the joint. You can think of synovial fluid as the oil for your body, smoothing your movements and protecting your bones from grinding against one another. Stretching and dynamic movement helps to get this synovial fluid back into the joint space which allows the bones to move more easily and safely, preventing injury as well as wear and tear on the bones.

When you stretch your body, you are relieving tight muscles and tension that builds up naturally in the body. Over time, you will find yourself becoming more flexible and you may even find that daily stretching increases your mobility. Daily tasks like walking, running, bending down, twisting and turning may become easier as you stretch and move your body. Remember, your body is designed to move. Embrace stretching as an easy and accessible way to add movement into your day.

Go to kerryfishercoaching.com for the video resource for this exercise.

PRACTICE

Note: This is a simple stretching routine that you can use during your Snooze Button Session. It will help you to stay limber and even more importantly, if it's been a while since you've stretched or moved your body in this way, this simple routine will help you to rediscover and reconnect with your body. Of course, if you already have a stretching routine, you could just as easily use that one during your snooze session.

Don't forget that we are lucky enough to live at a time when all the information we could ever need is at our fingertips; it's just a quick Google search away. Feel free to look up some stretching routines that target the areas you think you most need to work on. Remember, we have the most success when we make things our own, when we tailor them to our own lifestyle. This book is here to give you tips, tricks, and techniques but ultimately, you are your own teacher, and you must find what works for you.

Here's a quick countdown trick if you are having trouble getting out of bed. Tell yourself that you will jump out of bed when you reach the number one. Now, count backwards from five to one and when you hit the number one, you leap out of bed and maybe you add a shout of glee to reinforce your joy at getting up and doing your Snooze Button Session. Then, you begin your stretches.

Full Body Stretch

- Begin in a standing position with your arms at your side.
- Bring your arms to the side, up and around until they are above your head.
- Take a big stretch here, let your body stretch towards the ceiling.
- Lift one hand upwards as if you are reaching for the sky and then stretch the other arm upwards. Switch from side to side for three to five reaches on each side.
- Bring your arms down to your sides. Bring your arms out to the side, around and up to the sky. Let your palms come together at the top. Keep your palms together as you bring your hands down in front of you, ending at your chest. Repeat for three to five rounds.

Neck Rolls

Note: For this exercise, only roll your head in a half circle to the front.

- Stand with your arms by your side.
- On an exhale, bring your right ear to your right shoulder.
- On an inhale roll your head forward, bringing your chin to your chest.

- On an exhale, bring your left ear to your left shoulder.
- On an inhale, roll your head forward, bringing your chin to your chest.
- On the next exhale, bring your right ear to your right shoulder.
- Continue from side to side for three to five rounds.

Shoulder Rolls

- Stand with your arms at your side.
- On an inhale, raise your shoulders up towards your ears, trying to get your shoulders as high as you can.
- On an exhale, roll your shoulders forward and down in a semi-circle until your shoulders are all the way down.
- On an inhale, bring your shoulders back, around and back up to your shoulders.
- Continue for three to five rounds.
- Once you complete your forward shoulder rolls, reverse the direction for three to five rounds.

Arm Swings

Forward
- Stand with your feet hip distance apart, arms at your side.
- Inhale and bring your arms back, around and up above your head.
- Exhale as you bring your arms forward and down.
- Inhale as you bring your arms back, around and up above your head.
- Continue for five to ten rounds.

Back
- Remain in a standing position, feet hip distance apart.
- Inhale and bring your arms back, around and up over your head.
- Exhale and bring your arms forward and down.
- Inhale as you bring your arms back, around and up over your head.

- Continue for five to ten rounds.

Swinging Torso Twists

- Bring your arms out straight to your sides.
- Bend your knees slightly.
- Inhale as you swing to one side and exhale as you swing to the other.
- Keep swinging from side to side, slightly bending your knees as you twist from side to side.
- Link your breath to your movement, inhaling to one side and exhaling to the other,
- Repeat for 10-20 rounds.

Knee Lifts

- Stand with your feet hip distance apart. Bring your arms forward, straight out in front of you.
- Begin by lifting one knee and then the other, bringing the knees towards your outstretched arms.
- Keep lifting one knee after the other as you march in place.
- Feel free to add some extra movement here by actually moving around the room as you lift one knee and then the other.
- Complete 10-20 lifts per side.

Wide-leg Toe-touches

- Stand with your legs a little bit wider than hips distance apart. Make sure your legs are soft, with a slight bend (a micro-bend) in the knees.
- Bring your belly in to protect your lower back and spine and bend at the waist, reaching your right arm across your body and reaching for your left foot with your right hand.
- Come up to the halfway point, bringing your arm back up and out to the side, making sure that you keep your belly in and your back flat.

- Cross your left arm across your body and reach your left hand towards your right foot.
- Inhale as you reach to one side, exhale as you come up, inhale as you reach to the other side and continue on like this.
- Repeat for 10-20 rounds of touches, switching from side to side the whole time.

Go to kerryfishercoaching.com for the video resource for this exercise.

You don't have to be great to start,
but you have to start to be great.
—Zig Ziglar

EXERCISE 2: DYNAMIC STRETCHES—SEATED ROUTINE

Go to kerryfishercoaching.com for the video resource for this exercise.

Seated Wide Legged Stretch
- Sit on the ground with your legs stretched out in a wide legged seat, legs are straight.
- Stretch your arms out to the side and up towards the ceiling. Reach for the ceiling with first one hand and then the other. Arms remain straight.
- Bring your right arm out and over the right leg, allowing the arm to rest on the calf or knee as you lean towards the right, getting a nice side stretch. Your left arm swings up and next to your left ear.
- Bring your hands down onto the floor next to your outstretched right leg and then walk your hands until you are stretched forward, getting a nice forward fold stretch.
- Keep walking your hands along the ground, walking your hands until your left hand is on your left knee or calf and your right arm is up by your ear. Feel the nice side stretch here.

- Come up to center with your arms up above your head.
- Repeat this sequence beginning on the left side, finding the left side stretch and then walking your hands over to the center and then to the right for a side stretch there.
- Come back to the center. Repeat this sequence on each side one to three times.
- Bring your legs together with your toes flexed.

Seated Legs Together Stretch

- Inhale as you sit up very straight, getting your spine in alignment, chin is parallel to the ground, gaze is forward.
- Exhale as you bring your hands to either side of your outstretched legs, your right hand to the right and your left hand to the left. Begin to stretch forward, keeping your back straight.
- Inhale where you are, stretched out forward but straighten the spine once again.
- Exhale to move deeper into the forward fold.
- Keep going forward until you cannot go any further.
- At this point, you can round your back gently and bring your chin towards your chest.
- Enjoy the stretch for a few rounds of breath and then come back up to seated position.
- Repeat this one to three times.

Seated Side Stretches and Twists

- Bend your knees and come to a comfortable cross-legged seat.
- Inhale and bring your arms out to the side, around and up.
- Exhale as you bring your hands together in front of your chest in a prayer position.
- Repeat this circular arm motion three to five times, the arms come out to the side and around and up and then down the center of the chest with palms together.

- Link your breath to your movement, breathing in as your arms come up and around and breathing out as you bring your palms to your chest.
- Bring your right hand to the ground, tenting your fingers so that only your fingertips touch the ground, your palm is off the ground.
- Inhale as you stretch to the right side with your left arm going up and over your head to get a deep side stretch.
- Breathe here for a few rounds of breath.
- Inhale as you come up to center and then stretch your left hand down on the ground and your right arm comes up and over your head.
- Breathe here for a few rounds of breath.
- Continue for three to five rounds of side stretches.
- Inhale and twist to the right, allowing your right hand to come out and behind you slightly while the left hand holds your right knee.
- Breathe here for a few breaths, inhaling to release the pose a little and then exhaling as you twist deeper.
- Inhale and switch sides, allowing your left hand to come out and behind you slightly while your right hand holds your left knee.
- Repeat three to five rounds of twists.
- If you want to add some variety to this routine, you can do one side stretch to each side and then one twist to each side before returning to the side stretch on each side. Continue like this with the four stretches in a sequence.

If you want something you've never had, you must be
willing to do something you've never done.
—Thomas Jefferson

EXERCISE 3: QUICK, EASY, ACTIVE ROUTINE

Getting your body moving early in the morning is fantastic for your health and wellbeing. In this easy, accessible routine, you will be doing three simple exercises, one after the other, with a short ten-second break in between each exercise. You begin with a jumping jack, move to squats, and then push-ups. You will flow from exercise to exercise for the entire Snooze Button Session until the alarm goes off again. If you are unfamiliar with any of these exercises, make sure you google them so you have proper form.

PRACTICE

- Begin by jumping your legs out to the side, bringing your arms out to the side and up over your head. Continue for three sets of ten jumping jacks, pausing for ten seconds in between each set.
- Next, stand with your feet hips distance apart, arms at your side. Bend your knees and bring your straight arms out in front of you until they are parallel with the ground. Continue for three sets of ten squats, pausing for ten seconds in between each set.
- Finally, come to the ground and place yourself in a pushup position with your hands directly under your shoulders, your body in one long line, like a surfboard. Bend your elbows and bring your chest towards the ground. Continue for three sets of ten push-ups, pausing for ten seconds in between each set.
  - o You can do the push-ups with your knees up in the traditional position or if that is challenging, bring your knees down. Alternatively, you can do wall push-ups with your hands to the wall, feet slightly away from the wall and bend your elbows, bringing your chest towards the wall. As you get stronger, you can progress through the levels until you are doing the traditional push-up.
- Continue on in this circuit until the time is up. Push yourself to keep going for the entire Snooze Button Session.

Note: If you are struggling with this routine, keep with it. You will get stronger each day. If you do notice that this is a difficult routine to do, consider adding a couple of other rounds of this exercise throughout your day. Imagine the benefit of doing this three times per day, every day? The cumulative effect would be fantastic. Commit to your fitness and be amazed at what you can accomplish at any age.

Today I will do what others won't,
so tomorrow I can accomplish what others can't.
—Jerry Rice

EXERCISE 4: STRENGTH BUILDING ROUTINE

Beginning your day with active movement might be just what you need to get a great start to your day. You can use the movements below, look for a short routine on YouTube or make up your own. The idea is to do a little bit of light strength training even before you start your day. Studies have shown that a protein called BDNF, or brain derived neurotrophic factor is released when you exercise first thing in the morning.

BDNF is essential to the body. It helps to support neurons and brain cells and can even repair damaged brain cells. It is a protein that protects the brain from certain neurodegenerative diseases. BDNF also helps with long term memory storage and learning.

PRACTICE

Push-Ups
- Come to a push-up position with your knees up or down. This will depend on your strength.
- Bend your elbows and bring your body towards the ground, maintaining a straight body the whole way down. Imagine your body is a surfboard so you can keep it as straight as possible.
- Do ten push-ups and repeat for three rounds.

Lunges

- Stand with your arms at your sides,
- Step forward with your right foot and bend your knee to a 90-degree angle. Keep your left thigh parallel with the ground, if possible. Make sure that your right knee does not go past your right foot.
- Step back to the starting position.
- Repeat with your left leg.
- Make sure to keep your abdominal muscles engaged as you do your lunges. Keep your back straight, chin parallel with the ground, gaze forward.
- Continue moving from side to side, lunging with your right foot and then your left.
- Do one set of ten lunges on each side and repeat for one to three sets.

Squats

- Stand with your arms at your sides. Feet are hips distance apart, toes turned slightly outward.
- Bend your knees until your knees are parallel with the ground. As you bend, bring your arms up in front of you, parallel with the ground.
- Do one set of ten squats and repeat for one to three sets.
- You can also do squats using a ball. Put the ball between your back and the wall and bend and straighten your knees as you allow your back to roll on the ball. Do sets of ten squats, repeat for one to three sets.

To enjoy the glow of good health, you must exercise.
—Gene Tunney

EXERCISE 5: YOGA SUN SALUTATION A

Yoga has been practiced for thousands of years as a way of stretching and moving every part of the body. Yoga means "yoke" or unite.

The practice of yoga is to unite body, mind, and spirit. By moving your body along with your breath, you reconnect with your body and clear your mind.

Yoga was originally done as a way to prepare the practitioner for meditation so feel free to do one round of Sun Salutations for your first Snooze Session and then hit your snooze button and meditate for a second Snooze Button Session. This is the way you can begin to stack your practices and create a longer morning routine. This is called habit stacking and it is discussed in much more detail in a later chapter. For now, though, give it a try; do your yoga and then meditate. Two Snooze Button Sessions are so much better than one. I promise!

Go to kerryfishercoaching.com for the video resource for this exercise.

PRACTICE

- Stand at the front of your mat or at the front of the space you are in, leaving plenty of space behind you. Make sure your belly is in, legs are slightly bent (micro-bend).
- Inhale as you bring your arms to the side, around and up over your head.
- Exhale as you fold forward with a flat back, hands come towards the ground.
- Inhale as you come up halfway with a flat back.
- Exhale as you fold forward and bring your hands to the ground, stepping your feet out behind you into a push up position. Bend your elbows and come to the ground.
- Inhale as you bring your hands to either side of your chest, keep your gaze forward and down towards the ground as you arch your back upwards.
- Exhale as you bring your chest down, tuck your toes and come to a push up and then up and back into an inverted V, butt is up towards the place that the wall and ceiling meet. Push into

your hands, pressing your knuckles down. Keep your shoulders relaxed.

- Breathe here for three to five rounds of breath.
- Inhale to look up, exhale to step your feet to the front of your mat.
- Inhale to look up halfway and exhale to fold.
- Inhale all the way back up to standing position.
- This completes one round of sun salutation. Do three to five rounds each Snooze Button Session.

Yoga begins right where I am—not where I was
yesterday or where I long to be.
—Linda Sparrowe

EXERCISE 6: YOGA TABLETOP ROUTINE FOR SPINE HEALTH

Go to kerryfishercoaching.com for the video resource for this exercise.

- Come to your hands and knees, your hands are under your arms and your knees are under your hips.

Cat/Cow
- Inhale as you tuck your toes and drop your belly down towards the ground as your chin and butt lift towards the ceiling, gaze is forward and up. This is called cow position.
- Exhale as you round your back, chin comes towards your chest. This is called cat position.
- Do three to five rounds of cat-cow.

Cross-Armed Stretch
- Stretch your straight right arm towards the top left corner of the mat, your fingers are tented on the ground, fingertips down and

palm up. Pull your hips back on the diagonal towards the right side. Breathe here for three breaths.

- Switch sides by bringing your straight left arm towards the top right corner of your mat, fingers are tented on the ground, fingertips down and palm up. Pull your hips back on the diagonal towards the left side.

Lace Through Stretch

- Come back up to tabletop with your hands under your shoulders and your knees under your hips.
- Bring your straight right arm up, reaching your right hand towards the ceiling. Take a big inhale as you stretch deeply.
- Exhale as you lace your arm through, under your belly. Make sure you stay in tabletop position as your arm laces through.
- Inhale and stretch the arm up towards the ceiling, hand reaching up and lace through two more times.
- On the third lace through, allow your shoulder to land on the mat. The top of your head comes down, neck is relaxed. Breathe here for a few rounds of breath, enjoying the twist.
- On an inhale, stretch the arm upwards once more towards the ceiling before placing it down on the mat.
- Repeat on the other side with three lace-throughs with the left arm and then land with the shoulder on the mat and breathe for a few rounds of breath.
- Finish the sequence by doing three to five rounds of cat-cow.

Yoga is not a work-out, it is a work-in. And this is the point of spiritual practice; to make us teachable; to open up our hearts and focus our awareness so that we can know what we already know and be who we already are.
—Rolf Gates

EXERCISE 7: DANCING

You don't really need me to teach you how to dance, you naturally know how to dance. However, let me give you a few tips. First of all, pick music that you love. Then make sure that you release any inhibitions and allow yourself to simply move in a way that makes your body feel good. You might want to close your eyes to release any judgment of yourself and to get in touch with how you feel inside. Then, let loose and dance. Are you ready? Let's get ready to dance, dance, dance, dance.

PRACTICE

- Try dancing with your eyes closed to really get in touch with how you feel.
- Move along with the music and free yourself of any inhibitions, just dance.
- Remember to smile and have fun. Set yourself free.

HOW TO BRING MOVEMENT INTO YOUR DAY

Once you practice adding movement to your morning Snooze Button Session, you can begin to add movement to the rest of your day. Find times throughout the day that you can do five-15 minutes of movement and challenge yourself to move during those periods. A great way to do this is to add movement after each meal. After breakfast, you could take a quick walk; after lunch, add a walk or some light exercise and after dinner, you could take an evening stroll. If you really want to super-power your life, your body, and your fitness, do some light stretching before getting into bed at night, Make movement a regular and recurring part of your days.

Another way to add movement into your day is to take more frequent breaks during your workday. Every hour, get up and move around for five minutes. Even better, move for five minutes every half hour and see the difference it makes to your day, to your attitude and to your work quality. The Pomodoro Method advocates just this method for increasing productivity. Research from the University of Illinois shows that deactivating and reactivating work allows you to stay focused for a specific amount of time and then taking short, planned breaks. Another study from Kansas State University recommends the same thing, The study found that students were able to stay more focused if they planned what topic they would study and then took preplanned short breaks. During these breaks, you could jump on social media but how much better would it be for your body, mind, and spirit if you added movement during these breaks. Give it a try!

Here are some other ideas for increasing your movement. Take the stairs instead of the elevator. Park your car further from the store and walk the extra distance. Even better, leave your car home and bike or walk to work if that is a possibility. Take a walk in the park. Walk down your street and get to know your neighbors. When you get together with friends, consider doing an activity instead of going out to eat. Wherever you can, move, move, move.

If you still aren't convinced that adding movement to your life would be beneficial then I challenge you to do a one-week study of your habits. For one week, track how many hours a day you are active and how many hours per day you are inactive. You might be surprised with how many hours you are sedentary. This alone might motivate you to add movement to your day. So come on, get moving!

REFLECT

1. How do you feel on the days you exercise as opposed on the days when you are sedentary?

2. Begin to keep track of how many days per week you are doing strength training, cardiovascular exercises and stretching. Aim to have a variety of movement modalities in your mornings at least 5 days a week.

3. What works better for you? Stretching or exercise in the mornings?

4. What works best for you? Incorporating movement into your mornings or your evenings?

5. What active movement do you enjoy that you can bring into your days? Do you enjoy walking, hiking, biking, running, paddleboarding, playing tennis, basketball or another sport? Aim to incorporate fun activity into your life beyond your morning snooze sessions.

TO HUNCH OR NOT TO HUNCH, THAT IS THE QUESTION

As a peak performance and mindset coach who loves to study and learn about anatomy and movement, I am fascinated by the way people move and stand. I am always observing people and their movement patterns. Something I have noticed in the past ten years is that more and more people are standing in a hunched position with their heads out like a turtle. I always joke around with my kids that it seems like we learned to stand but now we are headed back down to the ground, onto all fours.

Who cares though? What does it matter? Well, one reason it matters is that the way we stand and move has a direct impact on your mind, your emotions. Notice now how you feel when you stand hunched over and how you feel when you stand tall with your chin up and your spine straight. I began experimenting with my students, teaching them this concept that the way we stand and move affects our emotional state and they came back and reported that they did notice a difference in their state of mind when they stood taller. They felt more confident, capable, and competent.

Listening to the feedback from my clients was super empowering and uplifting, and it made me focus even more on how our physical state affects our mental state. As I studied even deeper, I began to see that the MIND, the mental state also affects the physical state. It is a feedback loop. Truly, everything is connected. Body, mind, and spirit, all one.

> *I move, therefore I am.*
> —Haruki Murakami

*As we express our gratitude,
we must never forget that
the highest appreciation
is not to utter words,
but to live by them.*

—John F. Kennedy

CHAPTER 5

GRATITUDE

Wear gratitude like a cloak,
and it will feed every corner of your life.
—Rumi

I began a regular gratitude practice in the spring of 2019. I had read that *it was a practice that could change my life, so I decided to try it. I'll be honest, though, I wasn't a believer. In fact, I was highly skeptical about the practice, wondering why on earth feeling gratitude would change my life. I may be a skeptic, but I'm always willing to experiment, so I got a pretty journal, dubbed it my gratitude journal and began to write down ten things I was grateful for every day. I did this for almost a year. I didn't see much change in my life, and I certainly didn't feel any big emotional charge as I wrote my list of things I was grateful for, but nonetheless, I continued to write my lists each day.*

In March of 2020, the global coronavirus pandemic struck. I live in New York where the pandemic hit fast and furious. Within a period of three days, we went from worried about the pandemic to all events being canceled, schools closing down, and people frantically emptying the supermarkets, stocking up on all the food and toilet paper they would need for a global disaster. And then the world closed down. We were in a complete shutdown. The schools were closed, the roads were empty, everybody was cowering in their homes, scared and fearful of the future.

I remember it so clearly. It was the first day that my kids were home from school. The house was quiet, everyone still asleep. I grabbed my gratitude journal, went downstairs and got myself some tea. I went outside to sit in my backyard. It was still dark, with the slightest whispering of light beginning to peek above the horizon. The sky was gorgeous that day, streaked with oranges and yellows, pinks and purples. But even the sky couldn't keep the stress away that day.

I sat there thinking about what was going on. I felt the fear begin to well up in me. All the uncertainty and the craziness of the last days settled on me heavily, weighing me down. I felt the fear trying to pull me in, the emotional abyss beckoning to me. I looked at my gratitude journal and thought, "What the hell do I have to be grateful for right now? There's a global pandemic, the world has closed. There's nothing to be grateful for. Nothing."

With nothing to write, I opened my journal and began to leaf through the entries. I saw an entry where I had written that I was grateful for my kids. It stopped me short as I realized that four out of my five kids were home and the fifth was on his way. This was the first time in years that everybody would be together under one roof. The first time we would be a full family since my oldest had gone to college. The gratitude poured in. I DID feel grateful for this opportunity to have everyone together. I was grateful.

I turned to another page. On that list I had written that I was grateful for my home. As I sat in my backyard, looking around at the daffodils that were just starting to emerge from their long slumber in the ground, looking at our firepit and our barbecue and pool, I realized that I was super grateful for my home. What better place to be during a global pandemic? Plus, I had fully stocked my home weeks earlier when I first heard about the pandemic in China, just in case. So not only was my home beautiful and cozy and comfortable, but we could survive for months (maybe years, lol) with the supplies I had brought in. Gratitude flooded me as the feeling that I was safe, I was protected, all was well washed over me.

I turned to the last page and on that one, the first entry was that I was grateful for my breath. This one took my breath away for a moment. My breath had never seemed as important as it did at that moment, during a global pandemic where a respiratory illness was spreading like wildfire. I sat back and pondered my breath.

I experimented with taking some long, deep, relaxing breaths. The calmness and peace washed over me. Then I felt it, like a huge wave washing over me. I felt a wave of gratitude. It flooded my entire body.

As it did, my entire outlook changed. I was determined to make the pandemic a time of transformation for myself. I would transform myself, my home, my career, my life. And as I made this decision, I opened up the journal to a fresh new page and began to write what I was grateful for. This, my friends, is the power of gratitude. It can shift your entire outlook, change your entire life. As a matter of fact, tapping into that gratitude is what allowed me to realize that this was my opportunity to become the writer I had always dreamed of. This book is a direct result of my gratitude journal because I decided on that day, sitting outside on the first day of worldwide shutdown from a global pandemic, that I would stay positive, I would create, I would become. I would stay in a state of gratitude. Even now.

Gratitude is super powerful. It worked for me, and it can work for you too. So, come, let's learn about gratitude.

Gratitude has become a popular buzzword in recent years. Everyone is talking about feeling gratitude, expressing gratitude, and practicing gratitude. There are countless articles on how important it is to feel gratitude regularly and how you should embrace a way of living where you live in bliss and gratitude for everything around you. Now, I like a buzzword just as much as the next person but quite frankly, I wasn't sure that gratitude would truly be able to change my life. So I began to study gratitude and to learn about what the science says about gratitude.

I found an increasing amount of empirical research indicating that gratitude affects our well-being by training us to notice the positive emotions and events in our lives. Even more exciting, practicing gratitude has the effect of buffering us against negative states and emotions. This means not only does it make us feel great, gratitude protects us from the times when our lives become difficult or challenging. Gratitude can positively affect all areas of your life. Gratitude is associated with greater levels of happiness, and it has been shown to have a positive impact on your health and relationships.

The idea of feeling and expressing gratitude is a universal phenomenon that can be seen throughout history, expressed by all the major religious traditions throughout time. As long ago as 3,000 years ago, the Etruscans, an ancient civilization that flourished in Italy, had votive offerings in their temples. These offerings are very similar to the Milagros you see when you visit Mexico. The Milagros are miniature offerings shaped like body parts that are left at churches as a thank you for a healing that occurred.

In Christianity, gratitude means a person gives goodness and grace to all around them. These passages from the Bible illuminate the idea that being thankful, living in gratitude is a state to aspire to. "Give thanks in all circumstances; for this is the will of God in Christ Jesus for you." "This is the day that the Lord has made; let us rejoice and be glad in it." "Give thanks to the Lord, for God is good, for God's mercy endures forever." "And let the peace of Christ rule in your hearts, to which indeed you were called in one body. And be thankful." This idea is repeated throughout the scriptures. Here's one more: "Rejoice always, pray without ceasing, and give thanks in all circumstances." Notice, the idea is to give thanks in ALL circumstances, not just when positive events are happening. The idea is to live in a state of thanksgiving.

In Judaism, we find similar sentiments. Rabbi Brian Field illuminates us with this incredible concept. "Judaism is literally built upon gratitude. The original Hebrew word for Jew, *Yehudi*, is a form of the Hebrew word for thank you—*todah*. In other words, Judaism means "the path of gratitude." Instead of calling ourselves "the people of the book," we more accurately could call ourselves "the grateful people," "the people of the thank you." Pretty amazing, right? The religion is based on giving thanks. The Hebrew term for gratitude is *Hakarat Hatov* which literally means, "recognizing the good." Here are some Jewish prayers: "I thank you, living and enduring God, for you have restored my life to me: great is your faithfulness." And this one, said each morning upon awakening: "I thank You, living and eternal King, Who has returned my soul into me with compassion—great is Your faithfulness!"

For Muslims, there is Ramadan, an entire month dedicated to gratitude. During Ramadan, there is a month of fasting and prayer which culminates in a great feast. During Ramadan, charity is freely given. So beautiful, right? And here are some beautiful prayers that we should all be offering each day, "In the name of God the most Merciful the Beneficent. Oh Nourisher and Provider of all things. We offer our thanks and gratitude for this food, and for those who prepared it." "We offer our thanks and gratitude for each member of our community and the opportunity that we all have to come together to do good."

Gratitude plays a central role in the Buddhist religion. Buddhism emphasizes that thanks and prayers should be given for all the blessings but also all the suffering, the challenges, the obstacles. This quote says it all, "The Blessed One said, 'Now what is the level of a person of no integrity? A person of no integrity is ungrateful and unthankful. This ingratitude, this lack of thankfulness, is advocated by rude people. It is entirely on the level of people of no integrity. A person of integrity is grateful and thankful. This gratitude, this thankfulness, is advocated by civil people. It is entirely on the level of people of integrity'" (Katannu Sutta). Clearly gratitude is a main focus for Buddhists. Gratitude for all things is the way that Buddhists train their minds in order to prepare their spirits for enlightenment.

Hindus show gratitude in many small acts of hospitality and through service toward the divine presence, both in their homes and temple shrines. The Sanskrit term for gratitude is *Kritajna*. It comes from the word *krita* which means "cultivated" and *jna* which means "state of consciousness." How beautiful is that? Gratitude literally means a cultivated state of consciousness.

This is especially pertinent to our Snooze Button Sessions because the entire point of these early morning sessions is to get you to cultivate your state of consciousness. To shift your state of consciousness so you can begin to create the life of your dreams. It might seem impossible right now that you can change your entire life by taking a few minutes in the morning to meditate or exercise or practice gratitude but if you stick with me, by the end of this book, you will see significant changes in your life. You will begin to see a vision for what you can be. A vision of you as the next greatest version of yourself. But more on that later, for now, let's look at some of the Hindu prayers regarding gratitude.

Let's begin with the Kritajna Hum, "My true self is always grateful. I am connected with everything else in the universe. I am like an ocean—the deeper I go within, the more I connect with the stillness of my true self." The Dhanya Vad, "When I'm grateful, I find grace. By looking for the blessings in my life, I open up a space of light in every experience; I open up the path for grace to flow. I make room in the middle of everything for gratitude." And finally, the Ananda Hum, "When I gladden my heart, I awaken the energy of gratitude. This energy uplifts and expands me. By opening my heart, I can feel gratitude deeply. Gratitude shifts the moment by shifting me. Nothing around me changes; *I change.*" It is clear that any of these prayers could be used by anyone to bring a sense of gratitude into their life. Try one.

In the Muslim religion, three levels of gratitude, or thankfulness, are described. The levels progress from feeling grateful, to verbally expressing your gratitude to finally performing acts that show your gratitude. The first level is to realize and appreciate all of the blessings that you have. The next level is to actually begin to speak to others about how grateful you are for all your blessings. And then, it is time to do "righteous deeds" to express the gratitude you feel. An interesting fact is that the first chapter of the Quran starts with "'Alhamdulillah" which signifies gratitude in everyday life. Islam quite literally teaches an attitude of thankfulness from the moment you wake up until you go to sleep, for all your meals and drinks, for God. In other words, gratitude for everything in life. How beautiful is that?

Now that you know what some of the world religions say about gratitude, let's turn to some of the science behind gratitude. We can trace the idea of practicing gratitude all the way back to 1790. It was first mentioned by Adam Smith who regarded gratitude as an emotion that enhances social stability and serves as a moral barometer for behavior. It has been noted that when a person shows gratitude for another, there are grateful emotions in both parties, a benefit to both people.

There have been experiments which show that people will work harder when they are thanked for their efforts. Imagine that a simple thank you can inspire a person to do more than they would without the appreciation. Gratitude within relationships creates more fulfilling relationships. Expressing gratitude to others when they show kindness towards us helps to create a reinforcing loop where the same behavior is likely to be repeated in the future. This helps to strengthen relationships as the giving and the receiving partner are both receiving great reward.

Even more exciting is that training yourself to feel gratitude primes you to feel gratitude more frequently. It enables you to be able to feel gratitude in the future as well. Think of it like a muscle that you're building; a gratitude muscle. The more you use it, the stronger it grows. Once you begin to practice gratitude, you might find that you will have the added benefit of being able to experience other positive emotions more often as well.

A lot of research in the area of gratitude has been done by Dr. Robert Emmons of the University of California and Dr. Michael McCullough of the University of Miami. They conducted a study where students were randomly assigned to three groups for a ten-week period. The gratitude group described five things they were grateful for in the past week, the hassles group related five hassles they experienced in the previous week, and the events group related five events that affected them the previous week. After ten weeks, the study found that the students in the gratitude group felt more optimistic about their life than the participants in the other groups. The 2002 study supports the idea gratitude can have a true impact on well-being. McCullough et all write, "Highly grateful individuals tend to be more empathic, forgiving, helpful, and supportive as well as less focused on materialistic pursuits than are their less grateful counterparts."

Another highly interesting study in 2003 by Watkins and his colleagues devised a test called the GRAT (Gratitude, Resentment, and Appreciation) Test. This was a self-reported study where the participants reported whether they expressed and experienced gratitude, whether they felt abundant or deprived in their life, whether they appreciated the simple pleasures in life like seeing a flower or rainbow or beautiful sunset, and whether they expressed appreciation for the contributions others made for them. The study found there was a correlation between people who scored high on the GRAT test and higher levels of happiness and satisfaction in life.

Dr. Martin P. Seligman is a leading researcher and psychologist at the University of Pennsylvania. He is a leader in the field of positive psychology, and he did a fascinating assignment with students. He asked them to write a letter to someone who had been kind to them but whom they didn't ever thank for the kindness. He then had them personally deliver the letters. The participants had a huge increase in their happiness scores and this impact lasted for a month.

All of these studies indicate a connection between gratitude and well-being. I was convinced. It's one thing to read something and another to experience it, so I decided to start a gratitude practice and was surprised to find it actually had a major effect on me and on my life. I felt better, my thoughts were more positive, and I noticed that as I practiced gratitude, I began to see plenty of other things I was grateful for. Gratitude helped me, and I am confident it will help you which is why gratitude is one of the practices I want you to try during your Snooze Button Session.

Let's build an attitude of gratitude. Give it a try. You've got nothing to lose and a lot to gain! Who knows; it might even change your life.

IVAN'S STORY:
AN UNEXPECTED NEW YEAR'S EVE WITH GRATITUDE
DECEMBER 29TH, 2021.

Two days left until New Year's Eve. The enthusiasm was high and the plan for the party was done. Together with some friends, we would have dinner together and celebrate the arrival of the new year.

We would. But not.

On this day I received the unexpected news that one of the person's I had been in close contact with during the previous days tested positive for COVID-19. It was like a bucket full of ice had just fallen on me. Not only did I have the possibility of being infected myself, but it also meant I would spend the next few days at home, isolated—including New Year's Eve.

Honestly, I thought it would be a sad experience to be at home by myself, away from family and friends, during this festive moment. However, it turned out to be one of the most enjoyable, memorable and incredible New Year's Eve of my life.

Why? Simply because, by being by myself during this night, I fully enjoyed the moment like never before. While watching the fireworks near the bay, I was fully present in the moment. I looked back at the current year and thought about all the moments of learning, growth, joy, true happiness and Love I have lived. I appreciated the opportunities life has offered me and during the fireworks frenzy, only one word filled my mind and soul.

Gratitude. May we all be grateful for being alive and experiencing this wonderful journey we call Life.

BENEFITS OF GRATITUDE

Gratitude Improves:
- sleep
- resilience
- mental state
- empathy
- understanding
- compassion
- quality of relationships
- general state of well-being
- outlook on life
- self-esteem

Gratitude Reduces:
- feelings of depression
- stress
- loneliness
- aggression
- self-centeredness
- selfishness

LAWRENCE TUAZON'S GRATITUDE PRACTICE

Lawrence Tuazon is a good friend of mine whom I met through a personal growth platform called Mindvalley. From the moment I saw him appear in his zoom square and heard him speak, I knew I had to get to know him. He exuded a gentle, kind spirit, yet he's also a powerful, strong warrior.

I was fortunate that I had the opportunity to interview Lawrence and help him share his Hero's Journey. Once I heard his story, I was inspired and amazed, and I knew he was there to help a lot of people. Lawrence was on top of the world, had the job of his dreams, a family, all was going well when he had a terrible accident which eventually resulted in his leg being amputated. His long journey towards becoming the vibrant, ebullient, inspiring man he is today began with a gratitude practice. Here it is, in his own words.

LAWRENCE'S STORY

I chose Gratitude—the 1st thing that I learned to practice when I started my personal growth and development. I was in the hospital sitting in a wheelchair after a terrible accident when I first did this practice. I was asked to list 10 things in my life that I am grateful for.

I remember I was only able to list 3 things. The first thing I was grateful for was my family who were there by my side, all throughout my long hospitalization after the accident.

The second thing was that I was grateful for my wheelchair because it enabled me to move around when I couldn't walk after my right leg amputation surgery.

The third thing I was grateful for was the painkillers that I was given that diminished the pain of my leg temporarily.

At that point in my life, that was all I had, it all started from these three things. As time passed, I added things to my list and the list has grown into a thousand things that I am grateful for that are happening in my life right now that I am so grateful. I know eventually the list will be countless.

Gratitude can help us thrive especially in hard times. It gives me energy and healing to recover and brings me hope to start again with my life.

Gratitude practice totally changed my vision and perspective in life—a ripple effect to everything. I can easily see and recognize the opportunity in every situation.

It makes me rich; it makes me grow; it makes me whole. And I'm very grateful to the air that we breathe.

It makes us One.

THE EXERCISES

EXERCISE 1: GRATITUDE JOURNAL

Creating a dedicated gratitude journal that you keep right next to your bed may be exactly what you need. You can use a notebook, a beautiful journal you buy just for this purpose, or you can even use your phone or computer. You might want to try it both ways, one using a written method and then trying an electronic version. You want to pick a method that will be simple and that you will be able to stick with.

There have been some interesting studies done that indicate that a written practice may be beneficial. Studies done at Princeton University and UCLA indicated that physically writing information with pen and paper allowed the writer to develop a stronger conceptual relationship with the writing. The study also established that students who took notes by hand had much better comprehension and recall than those people who used their computers to take notes *(Mueller & Oppenheimer, 2014)*. Handwriting has been shown to boost long term memory, enhance creativity, and boost recall. Give it a try; see how a handwritten gratitude practice feels for you.

PRACTICE

- When your alarm goes off, grab your journal and pen and begin to write a list of ten things you feel grateful for. Try to write down ten things each day and don't overthink it. Write freely, allowing your mind to be relaxed and calm. Allow the ideas to flow through you without thought.
- Look at the list when you are done and pick out one thing that you are grateful for. Close your eyes and form a picture in your head of what you are grateful for. If you are grateful for your children, see a picture of your kids in your mind's eye. If you are grateful

for your job, imagine your office and your coworkers. Whatever you are grateful for, create a picture of it and try to immerse yourself in this vision. Feel the feelings that you associate with this thing you are grateful for. Allow the feelings to flow into your body and smile. Feeling the emotion is the most important part in terms of truly experiencing the benefits of gratitude practice.

- If you have trouble visualizing or forming pictures in your head, don't worry. Just imagine the feeling of the thing that you are grateful for. Allow the feelings to simply come in and wash over you.
- Feel free to write the same things down each day, make a fresh list each day or do a combination, some new things, some repeated.
- If you have time, pick a second thing from the list and think about how grateful you are for that. Again, allow the emotions to flow throughout your body, intensifying them as much as possible.
- Continue picking something from your list and feeling gratitude until the alarm rings. At that point, you can begin your day or maybe, just maybe, you are feeling so grateful that you hit the snooze button one more time and continue practicing gratitude.
- If you are really feeling motivated during your second Snooze Button Session, make a second list of ten things you are grateful for, challenging yourself to write a completely new list. Imagine being grateful for 20 things before your feet even touch the floor! Now that, my friends, is a great Snooze Button Session!

There is a calmness to a life lived in gratitude, a quiet joy.
—Ralph H. Blum

EXERCISE 2: GRATITUDE VISUALIZATION

In this exercise, you will visualize all the things you are grateful for. You begin by feeling gratitude towards yourself, then you move to feeling gratitude for your relationships, then your career and finally, you feel gratitude for your life. This is a great practice because it allows you to survey many areas of your life and to feel gratitude for all the things that are going right in your life.

Go to kerryfishercoaching.com for the video resource for this exercise.

PRACTICE

- Hit the Snooze Button.
- Sit up straight in bed and take a deep breath in and a long, slow breath out.
- Begin by relaxing the top of your head, your forehead, your cheeks, corners of your eyes, corners of your mouth. Relax your shoulders, arms, hands and fingers. Relax your chest and back, belly and low back. Let your hips feel heavy. Relax your legs, your feet, your toes.
- Take a deep breath in and a long, slow breath out.
- Think of three things you are grateful for about yourself.
- Ideas: Be grateful for your good health, your looks, beautiful eyes or hair, your personality, your sense of humor, your intelligence, your kindness, your ability to work hard, your compassion, your ability to love.
- What are the things about you that are really special? If you have trouble with this one, then list five things you are grateful for about yourself. There's only one of you, it's time to start appreciating how special you really are.
- Think of three things that you are grateful for about your relationships.
- Ideas: Think of the people you have in your life. Your parents, children, extended family, neighbors, friends, acquaintances, coworkers, the people you meet in stores and restaurants.
- Which relationships do you have that create a sense of joy and exuberance in your life? Remember all the amazing people you have in your life.

- Think of three things that you are grateful for about your career.
- Ideas: Do you love your work? Are your coworkers amazing? Do you have great people you interact with due to your work? Does your career really fulfill you? Do you have a great boss? A great business?
- What are the things that are truly spectacular about your job? It might be helpful to remember why you started that career in the first place, why you were attracted to that job. Get back in touch with the pleasures of your job.
- Think of three things that you are grateful for about your life.
- Ideas: Your house, your ability to travel, your hobbies, your adventuring. Your neighborhood. Your country. Your car. Your friends. Your family. Your good health.
- Think about all the blessings you have in your life and allow the emotion of gratitude to flood your body. Allow your mind to embrace all aspects of your life as you think about what you have to be grateful for.

Gratitude is a powerful catalyst for happiness. It's the
spark that lights a fire of joy in your soul.
—Amy Collett

EXERCISE 3: GRATITUDE MEDITATION

Imagine if you had a personalized gratitude meditation tailored to you? Well, here is your chance to have just that! This one takes a little bit of prep work the day or night before you begin your Snooze Button Practice. You will be using your phone or computer to record yourself as you say all the things you are grateful for. Remember, this is just for you, so make sure that you really put your heart, soul, and emotions into it. This might just become your favorite meditation! Look at you! Just a few chapters ago, you were just adding meditation into your daily life and now here you are creating your very own meditation. Now that, my friends, is progress!

For inspiration, you can check out the resources section for a link to a gratitude meditation that I made for you to use as a model.

CREATE YOUR GRATITUDE MEDITATION

1. Put on some relaxing music and then take out your phone and press record.
2. Begin by saying this...relax the top of your head, relax your forehead, relax the corners of your eyes, relax the corners of your mouth. Take a deep breath in and a long slow breath out. Allow the feeling of relaxation to wash down over your shoulders, your torso, your hips, all the way down your legs, feet, and toes. Take a deep breath in and a long breath out.
3. Next, say...
    a. What are the things that you are grateful for about yourself?
    b. What are the things that you are grateful for about your career?
    c. What are the things that you are grateful for about your life?
4. Make sure you pause in between each question so that when you are listening and practicing along with your meditation, you will have time to mentally answer the questions and list what you are grateful for.

CREATIVE VISUALIZATION GRATITUDE PRACTICE

1. Make sure you have your phone right outside your bedroom door (not in your room but that's a topic for my next book so for now, you can leave it wherever you want. But outside your bedroom is preferable).

2. When the alarm goes off, press the Snooze Button and retrieve your phone and sit down. Play your gratitude recording.
3. Keeping your eyes closed, follow along with the meditation. Let the images come to your mind along with your recording. If you have difficulty visualizing, simply list the things that you are grateful for in each category.
4. Remember to feel the emotions that arise as you think about all the things that you are grateful for. Intensify the emotions as much as you can.
5. Note: You can do this exercise as a creative visualization exercise as it is written or you can grab your gratitude journal and listen to your gratitude meditation and journal along with the melodious sounds of your own voice. How great does that sound?

Some people grumble that roses have thorns;
I am grateful that thorns have roses.
—Alphonse Karr

EXERCISE 4: GRATITUDE NOTES

Another way to practice gratitude is to write a gratitude note to someone you love and appreciate and then give the note to them. This is one of the most beautiful ways to spread love and gratitude throughout your world. Imagine how you would feel if someone gave you a handwritten note or sent you an email or text telling you how grateful they are for you. It would make your day, right? So why not do this for someone else?

You can write to someone who did something kind for you. You can write to someone who you absolutely love and who you want to tell how much you appreciate. You can write a note of gratitude for a person who works in a store you frequent or your mailman or the garbage collectors. You can write a note of gratitude for your children or parents. You can even write a note for a neighbor or friend. It is such a simple thing to spend a few minutes writing a note to someone whom you love, expressing what you love about them. The pleasure is twofold. First, it is enjoyable to write the note and then it is even more enjoyable to give the note to the person. That is called a win-win. And who knows, you might even start a kindness revolution!

PRACTICE

Hit the Snooze Button and grab some paper or your phone or computer. Think about someone you appreciate and begin to write. Write whatever comes to mind, quickly and without censoring yourself. Just let the words pour straight from your heart onto the paper.

Once you have finished writing, you can send it if it is electronic or if it is a written note, then place it in an envelope and remember to either mail it or hand deliver it to the person.

If you have time, you can hit your Snooze Button a second time and write another note. If you are enjoying it, write a few notes to the people in your life who make your life great. It is a great way to start your day, spreading gratitude to all those you love. How can your day be anything but great once you begin it that way?

> *I don't have to chase extraordinary moments to*
> *find happiness—it's right in front of me*
> *if I'm paying attention and practicing gratitude.*
> —Brene Brown

HOW TO BRING GRATITUDE INTO YOUR DAY

Ok, here is your chance to weave gratitude into the fabric of your life. Think of gratitude as a muscle you are training, a gratitude muscle. The more you train it, the more gratitude you will feel. Before you know it, you will be finding more and more things to be grateful for. Remember Lawrence's story? At first, he only had three things to be grateful for but the more he practiced it, the more things he found to be grateful for. That's how gratitude works; it is like compounding interest. The more you practice, the more it grows.

The easiest way to bring gratitude into your life is to practice gratitude before or after every meal. Make this into a habit. In many cultures, this is already woven into the fabric of life; the practice of giving thanks before you eat. Why not bring it into your life? It's easy to remember because we all have to eat, so this is one of the best ways to add more gratitude into your day.

Another beautiful practice is to practice gratitude as you eat. Find a time that you can eat alone, uninterrupted. Sit down with your food and look at your plate, your utensils, your glass, your napkin. Feel gratitude for the people who made those items, the people who shipped those items, the people who sold those items.

Next, look at your food and take a moment to inhale deeply, appreciating the delicious scent of your food. Look closely at your food and see how beautiful it is. Begin to think about all the people who helped to get that food onto your plate. If you are eating fruits, vegetables, grains, or rice, think about the farmer that planted the crops, the workers who picked the crop. If you are eating processed foods, think about the factory owner who decided to build the factory, the workers who built the factory and those who work inside the factory. Think about the truckers who brought the product to market and the people who unpacked it and put it on the shelves in your local supermarket. Take another moment to appreciate all the people in the chain that helped to get that food onto your plate. It is truly incredible.

When it is time to go to work, let yourself look forward to the day and feel gratitude that you have a job. Feel grateful that you are able to work, that you are able to make a living and support yourself. Be grateful for the people at work, your building, the office you work in, and the desk you sit at. Be grateful that you have a computer to work on and a place you go each day to be productive. Go in with the air of gratitude, smiling at everyone you pass. Bring that feeling into your workplace and see the magic that unfolds.

Finally, remember to compliment people if you see something they are doing that is admirable or kind or if they are especially sweet. If you notice someone has beautiful eyes, a great smile, or that they're in amazing shape, compliment them. You can compliment someone's clothing, their car, their style, their grace. Express gratitude for anyone you interact with throughout the day—the store clerks, the gas station attendant, the waiter or waitress, the bank teller, the people on your zoom call. Whenever you have the opportunity to give an honest, sincere compliment, go for it. Life becomes beautiful when you go through life like this. Try it and watch as your entire life fills with joyous wonderment, fun, and happiness. This is the way you can light up every room you enter, enlivening it with your generous, grateful spirit. Give it a try. It will change everything.

> *I don't have to chase extraordinary moments*
> *to find happiness—it's right in front of me if I'm*
> *paying attention and practicing gratitude.*
> —Brene Brown

REFLECT

- When could you add some gratitude into your life? Pick one of the "bringing the practices into your day" suggestions and commit to trying it for one week.
- How do you feel as you think about or write about the things that you are grateful for?
- Notice when you have a negative thought and immediately replace it by thinking about something you feel grateful for.
- Find a lucky pebble or small stone and place it into your pocket and every time you feel it, think of one thing you are grateful for. Reflect on how this makes you feel throughout the day.

Joy is the simplest form of gratitude.
—Karl Barth

GRATITUDE LIST

Your breath	Your family
Your body	Your mind
Your intelligence	Your pets
Your home	Your bed
Books	Nature
Music	Art
Movies	Sex
Life	Sun, moon, stars
Meditation	Exercise
Beauty	The world

Whatever we think about and feel
grateful for expands.
—Kerry Fisher

Forgiveness is the fragrance that the violet sheds on the heel that has crushed it.

—MARK TWAIN

CHAPTER 6

FORGIVENESS

The weak can never forgive.
Forgiveness is the attribute of the strong.
—Mahatma Gandhi

*W*hen I was two years old, my parents got divorced, and my dad moved far away to start a new family. I was left feeling unmoored and disconnected from him which led to a lifetime of struggle with my feelings for my father. I spent many years blaming my dad for leaving me and went through long periods where I had little or no contact with him. I was angry. It was impossible for me to ever forgive him for what he had done. The pain in my heart was unbearable.

Then, one day, I started to learn about forgiveness and understanding. I realized that this was the path to freedom. I began the process to understand my father and once I did, I felt a lightening, a lifting of the burden I had carried for so long in my life. By understanding my dad, I was finally able to forgive him, finally able to let the past go. By forgiving my dad and understanding him, I opened the doorway to a place where I am now, no longer held by the pain of the past. I am free.

Forgiveness is a challenge for me which is why I am writing this chapter. I wanted to make sure to challenge myself and to do the work alongside you. So here I am. My most challenging area—forgiveness.

I have been working on forgiveness my entire life. It took me many, many years to finally understand how important it was to apply forgiveness towards every person I had ever held a grudge against. I had to learn to apply forgiveness to anyone I had even a minor negative feeling about.

I discovered that forgiveness is a result of learning to understand others. It is through understanding another person—who they are and the journey which brought them there—that you make it less about you, and you begin to open up towards them. Once you discover a person's story, you have a greater chance to develop more empathy towards them. More empathy leads to the ability to take someone else's perspective. In other words, it gives us the ability to understand others. This is how understanding opens up the door towards forgiveness. Forgiveness isn't always easy but because of the level of connection it creates between people, it is always worth it because having negative thoughts toward another person affects them a lot less than it affects the person with the resentment. Often one person will feel a massive weight of resentment towards another person, and the other person doesn't even know it. Their lives are unchanged, but the individual with the resentment is oppressed by anger and other negative emotions.

To get right down to it, why would you even want to forgive someone else? Especially, if they've caused you massive amounts of pain. The answer may surprise you. By forgiving someone else, you actually free yourself. Forgiveness is often seen as something we do for others, as if we're doing them a favor. In truth, forgiving others is the greatest gift you can give yourself.

There is a five-day program called 40 Years of Zen, which involves, amongst other things, hooking participants up to a very hi-tech electroencephalograph (EEG) and monitoring their brain waves. Of the information that is gathered during numerous sessions, there is a lot of emphasis placed on alpha brain waves. Alpha brain waves are particular brain waves which studies show are related to love, creativity, compassion, and insight. It is no accident that high amounts of alpha brain waves are typically found in Zen monks who have been meditating for up to 40 years. The most interesting thing that came out of the research from this program was that more than anything else, the one practice which causes a significant spike in alpha brain waves is forgiveness. Crazy, right?

During the 40 Years of Zen program, participants spend a week sitting in a "pod" forgiving every single person who has ever wronged them, from the smallest offender all the way up to the people who hurt them the most deeply. Then, participants review their brain wave patterns to determine the correlation between their alpha waves and the level of forgiveness they were able to achieve. So quite literally, the more you forgive, the more loving you become, and the more profound your personal insights. Best of all, most participants report feeling an increased sense of freedom and lightness after just a week of forgiveness. Program participants also notice massive improvements in the function of their brain that is reflected in how they show up and perform in their personal and professional lives. Imagine that? Forgiveness releases your energy, clears your mind, and sets you free to be the best version of yourself.

On his experience participating in the 40 Years of Zen program, Mindvalley founder Vishen Lakhiani says, "What I got out of the 40 Years of Zen project was 'freedom.' The thing that made this the most powerful personal growth experience I'd ever had was the sense of liberation I felt at the end of it. I had cleaned myself of so many grudges I had held onto for years. I was able to let go of painful memories I had forgotten I even had. And, I finally released the charges against people who I believed wronged me in my life. Today, I have never felt more at peace with myself."

BENEFITS OF FORGIVENESS

Forgiveness Improves:
- immune system
- mental health
- self-esteem

- relationships
- heart health
- feelings of happiness
- energy levels

Forgiveness Reduces:
- depression
- anxiety
- stress levels
- suffering
- resentment
- negative emotions
- sadness

THE EXERCISES

EXERCISE 1: JOURNALING

The first exercise takes place over two days and involves journaling. Since you are doing this in the morning as soon as you wake up, it would be helpful to have your journal next to your bed or in a bedside drawer. As soon as you hit the snooze button, begin to journal.

Day 1
- Make a list of every single person you are currently holding a grudge against, anyone you are upset with, and/or anyone you believed has ever wronged you.
- Include everyone you can think of including the people who may have only crossed your path briefly, like the guy who cut you off on the road, or the lady who gave you a dirty look.
- Now that you have this list, take a look at it. Each one of these people represents an opportunity for you to let go of some blocked

emotion and regain any energy you may have blocked. It might seem simple, but it actually works.

Day 2

- Pick one person on your list from the previous day as your point of focus during this practice. If you have never done forgiveness work before, start with someone who is relatively easy to forgive.
- Envision the person you want to forgive in front of you.
- Write down all the things you would like to forgive them for. Describe the items as if you were a judge reading charges to them in a court of law.
- Let yourself feel the full emotion you feel towards the person as you write it all down.
- After writing everything down, set a timer for three minutes and allow yourself to feel all of the emotions.
- When the timer sounds, immediately drop all the emotions you are feeling (this may be difficult but do your best). Imagine you can wipe the slate clean.
- Now, write possible reasons that the person might have done whatever it is that offended or hurt you. Try to understand their point of view or what could have happened to them for them to treat you that way. Journal as much as you can, letting the feelings of release wash over you as you write.
- Notice how you feel as you write.
- If you can forgive the person, do so now by writing that you forgive them and set them free.
- You might need to revisit this person a few times before you can fully remove any charge you have with that person.
- You can move on to the next person on your list when you are ready. Continue to work through the list for the next few days/weeks/months until you are able to feel clean and clear towards all the people on your list.

- When you have completed going through your entire list, this is the moment you set yourself free and regain all the lost energy you have left with them for all those years.
- You might need a few snooze sessions for this to fully work.
- Make sure you begin by forgiving someone who didn't do anything terrible to you. It might be the person who cut you off on the road or your child who was being rude to you. Maybe a waitress was rude or the guy at Starbucks who made your coffee badly. Start with the small stuff and work up to the people who are more difficult to forgive. Before you know it, you will be a forgiveness pro.

If we really want to love, we must learn how to forgive.
—Mother Teresa

EXERCISE 2: FORGIVENESS VISUALIZATION

This is a visualization exercise. The practice is very similar to the journaling practice above but in this exercise, you simply imagine the person with you and then walk through the forgiveness and understanding practice. This is based on a guided forgiveness meditation by Vishen Lakhiani. You can find this online by searching under his name. While you are there, you might want to check out some of his other videos and his educational platform called Mindvalley. It will change your life. I know, it changed mine, But I digress. Back to the exercise:

Go to kerryfishercoaching.com for the video resource for this exercise.

Here Are the Steps
- **Get comfortable**. If you would like, play some calming background music.
- **See the person**. Imagine the person you want to forgive. See them standing in front of you. Allow any and all feelings to come up within you.

- **Read the charges.** Tell the person how you feel; say all the things you want to say to them. Really feel the emotions as they come up.
- **Stop and release the emotions**
- **See the person.** Really see them for who they are and begin to have a curiosity about them. Who are they? How did they become the person you see standing there? What might have occurred in their life that made them show up as they did in yours.
- **Reach for understanding.** Go easy on yourself here. It might take a few tries before you reach true forgiveness. Let the process unfold naturally. If you reach understanding, then perhaps you can go to the next step. If you cannot reach understanding yet, be ok with that and simply try again another time with this person.
- **Forgiveness: Forgive into Love** Let's imagine the person and forgive them. Perhaps say the words as you gaze at them in your mind's eye. If you feel comfortable, give them a hug. Release the charge you have towards them, set yourself free, and set them free.
- Breathe, relax, reflect.
- Journal if it feels appropriate.

EXERCISE 3: FORGIVING YOURSELF

If you really want to get serious about forgiveness, then begin to practice forgiving the person you need to forgive most but whom you typically forgive least. Yes, I am talking about forgiving yourself. Forgiving yourself is not a practice for the meek, for the faint of heart. It is often one of the hardest things you can do, but it is also the one that will set you free.

Do the above meditation but instead of thinking of someone else to forgive, imagine yourself standing there in front of you. Imagine yourself as you were the age you were at the time you need to forgive. See yourself wearing the clothing you wore, with the haircut you had, looking just as you did in the past. Go through the entire forgiveness exercise and make sure that you read all the charges fully. Allow all your deepest, darkest feelings arise as you tell the younger version of you how you feel about their actions.

Then stop and really look at the younger version of yourself. Really see that younger you. Why did they do what they did? What happened in their childhood, in your childhood, that created the situation that happened? Feel empathy and compassion for the acts of your younger self. Then take a deep breath and forgive into love. Hug the younger version of you in your mind's eye. Release the guilt, the shame, the anger, the embarrassment. Let it all go.

Another self-forgiveness practice you can try comes from Lisa Nichols, an incredible speaker, teacher, and leader. She talks about how she did this practice for months, and it utterly changed her life. It is powerful and quite emotional but it works.

PRACTICE

- Stand in front of a mirror and gaze deeply into your own eyes.
- As you hold your own gaze, fill in these statements, completing each one by adding seven endings to each sentence.
- I forgive myself for...(fill in seven different endings for this).
- I am proud of myself that...(again fill in seven endings).
- I commit to myself that...(add seven endings here).
- Do this practice once a day, or even twice a day, every day for 30 days.

How unhappy is he who cannot forgive himself.
—Publilius Syrus

EXERCISE 3: HO'OPONOPONO EXERCISE

Ho'oponopono is an ancient practice of reconciliation and forgiveness utilized across the South Pacific Islands from Hawaii to New Zealand,

Tahiti, and Samoa, predicated on the idea that we must right any wrong we have committed. This is a simple yet profoundly beautiful practice.

Go to kerryfishercoaching.com for the video resource for this exercise.

PRACTICE

- Get comfortable, go into a meditative state and then simply begin with these words: I'm sorry. Please forgive me. Thank you. I love you.
- If you want to go a little deeper, you can use each sentence and fill in the blank like this:
- I'm sorry for hurting you.
- Please forgive me for not being there for you.
- Thank you for helping me see my missteps.
- I love you very much.
- You can also do this practice by filling in the blanks for specific purposes that are important to you:
- I'm sorry I lost my temper and yelled at you, Joe.
- Please forgive me for saying those hurtful things, Joe.
- Thank you for understanding that I am human, and I truly regret this, Joe.
- I love you, Joe.
- You can do this as many times as it feels comfortable throughout the day or over a period of time.
- You can repeat it twice a day, once in the morning and once in the evening until any emotional charge you feel towards the other person is gone.

We must develop and maintain the capacity to forgive.
He who is devoid of the power to forgive
is devoid of the power to love.
—Martin Luther King, Jr., A Gift of Love

EXERCISE 4: WHAT'S SO FUNNY ABOUT PEACE, LOVE, AND UNDERSTANDING?

That's a great song by Elvis Costello. It's also a great motto for life. Here I issue a challenge: I challenge you to keep practicing forgiveness until you have forgiven every single person you have to forgive, including yourself, the person who is often the hardest person to forgive. Once you have done that, once you have freed up the energy that has been bound up in these negative emotions in your body, you are ready for an advanced practice. This, my friends, is bonus material, and it is what I call a "Tool of Gold."

> *Understanding replaces forgiveness*
> *in the mind of a master.*
> —Neale Donald Walsch

The practice of understanding is a practice that we get to once we are experts at forgiving. Once we are at the point where something happens and we immediately forgive the person or event or ourselves, we are ready to move onto the practice of understanding. I know, I know, you aren't understanding what all this talk about understanding is yet, but bear with me. This is a true game changer.

You see, we can actually move to a place where we no longer need to forgive anyone. I know, I know; it seems impossible, but it isn't. Just like anything, it's a skill we can get better at with practice and time. To begin, we start to notice when someone or something upsets us. Then we think to ourselves, "Is there a time that I have done something like that?" Or, we think, "Can there be a reason other than the one I am imagining for this behavior?" We begin to look for reasons for the actions of others, for the events in our lives. And as we do, we take the charge out of the person or activity before it even builds up. We don't need to forgive because we understand. We have replaced forgiveness with understanding. Just like a true master.

PRACTICE

- As soon as you hit the snooze button, think of a person who offended you or hurt your feelings.
- Think about what your original thoughts were about why the person did this.
- Now, imagine a giant eraser that comes and erases all those thoughts and judgements.
- Think of the person and what they did and make up a few reasons why they did it that are more positive. For instance, if someone cut you off on the road, you can imagine that they were rushing to their child's soccer game or they were running to see their mother in the hospital. If one of your friends hurts your feelings, you might think that maybe they are going through a hard time themselves or perhaps they simply didn't realize their words would hurt you.
- Keep practicing this skill of thinking of alternate reasons for the actions of others. This simple practice is highly effective at taking away a lot of negative emotions that you might experience. Try it during your Snooze Button Session and then try it during your day. Soon enough, you shall be a master!

HOW TO BRING FORGIVENESS INTO YOUR DAY

Doing a forgiveness practice first thing in the morning is a truly life changing practice. By starting your day this way, you set yourself up for a day filled with understanding and love.

Throughout your day, anytime something happens that makes you have any negative feeling at all, simply notice it and then use empathy to forgive the person by thinking, "I have been in a situation when I have acted that way too. I forgive you."

You will be amazed at how easy it is to do this once you train yourself. Remember this: people typically aren't trying to upset you. They are having their experience and sometimes that affects you. But *it's not about you.*

Take a very simple example of someone who cuts you off on the road. As it happens, it can make you angry. But haven't you been in that situation when you were in a rush and did something similar, either deliberately or by mistake? Of course, you have. Remember that next time. Whatever a person is doing, you have most likely done something similar at some point in your life. And just as you would expect people to forgive you, you should forgive them.

A really great thing to do as you go through your day is to try to think of alternate reasons the person did what they did to offend you. In the example of the person cutting you off, it could be that they are late for work, having a medical emergency, or a family emergency. We give meaning to things and believe that is the true story, but we don't really know if it is. Better to think of reasons that don't make you angry than ones that do.

Before you go to bed at night, go through your day and forgive everyone you need to forgive.

As you practice immediate forgiveness for the way anyone ever treats you, you might even move to a state where you don't even have to forgive them because you understand them before you get angry. Be sure to forgive often and don't forget to forgive yourself too.

True forgiveness is when you can say
'Thank you for that experience.'
—Oprah

FINAL THOUGHTS

Forgiveness is one of the most impactful practices you can bring into your life. It is quite literally a game changer. A life-changer. And while it would be amazing to actually contact every single person who ever harmed you and every single person you ever hurt, it might not be practical. The great thing is that you can have the same exact results without ever contacting the people involved. This means you can ask for, as well as give, forgiveness to any person, no matter where they are in this world and even those who are no longer in this world. Imagine that!

It sounds crazy, but it is true. You see, the most important thing with forgiveness is that you release that block you have inside of you, usually in your mind, that still holds the residue of the interaction which did not go well in your life. Without releasing this, resentment acts as a weight in your body. You have the power to release this weight as soon as you recognize that forgiving others is one of the best things you can do to free yourself.

In the end, what kind of forgiveness are we talking about and to whom? The answer is simple—give forgiveness to every single person you have ever had a negative interaction with.

Start small—the person who cut you off in traffic, the person who took your parking spot. Then, maybe the salesperson who was rude or a person you passed on the street who gave you a dirty look. Then, move to the more difficult situations.The situations that were really painful, and the people whom perhaps you don't even want to forgive. Yes, those people. The ones who really, truly hurt you down to your very core. Your friends who were not there for you, your parents (I think everyone has some forgiveness to give to their parents), siblings, extended family members, a boss who treated you unfairly. Go through the list, one by one, and imagine the person, remember the situation, feel the pain from that situation. And now, forgive them. And ask them to forgive you. Yes, that's right, since there are always two sides to every story, it is likely that the person who you perceived to have hurt you also feels hurt by how you acted in that negative situation.

Remember that the person you most need to forgive is yourself. Look yourself in the mirror each day and gaze deeply in your eyes and say all the things you forgive yourself for. Do the forgiveness exercises detailed above and forgive every single thing that you have ever done that you regret. Forgive yourself for doing those things that you wish you could take back or feel embarrassed about and remind yourself that you were younger then. You didn't know any better, you did the best you could at that time. Forgive yourself and set yourself free. Don't you deserve that? Yes, you do.

ENCOURAGEMENT

This exercise is not for the faint of heart. This is seriously difficult work. You have to reach in, pull out those painful incidents that perhaps you prefer to keep buried, and then absolve the other person and yourself of any guilt, blame, or negative feelings.

Simply say, "Please forgive me for anything I did to harm you." Or, "I forgive you for anything you did to harm me." Truly see the person, look at them in your mind's eye as you do this exercise. It doesn't have to only be serious wrongs that were done to you, but anything that struck you as negative. Here's a good clue to consider—if you keep thinking about it, then it needs to be addressed.

Forgiveness is a funny thing.
It warms the heart and cools the sting.
—William A. Ward

REFLECT

- Who are some of the people you need to forgive from your childhood? Family? Friends? Teachers? Make a list.
- Who are some of the people you need to forgive from your adult life? Family? Friends? Professors? Significant other? Coworkers? Bosses?
- How do you feel when you think about the person who wronged you?

- How do you feel after you do one of the forgiveness exercises? How does your body feel? How does your mind feel? How does your spirit feel? Is there a sense of lightness or lifting?
- Who is the one person whom you need to forgive to set yourself free?

THE HARDEST PERSON TO FORGIVE

I was on a live call, listening to a forgiveness meditation by Vishen Lakhiani. As I listened to his soothing voice asking me to conjure up a picture of a person that I needed to forgive, the person who jumped into my mind was me. I needed to forgive myself. As I realized this, I felt a sharp pain in my chest and a throbbing in my temples. My cheeks flushed and my heart started to beat really fast.

Forgive myself? Really? Why would that bring such an immediate and extreme reaction I wondered? What did I need to forgive myself for, anyway?

After the call I felt preoccupied, out of sorts. I sat outside and thought about forgiving. myself and what I had to forgive. The answers came tumbling in. One after the other, the thoughts flooded my mind, listing all the things I thought I needed to forgive myself for. There were a lot of them. Suddenly, as I sat pondering this question, my thoughts stopped and I had a very vivid picture in my mind of a younger version of myself. I realized that this was the version of me that I needed to forgive. The young woman I once was.

Why? Well, that Kerry, the younger me, really wanted to be loved. She really wanted to be like everyone else, to fit in. And because she needed and wanted that so badly, she made a lot of decisions that were contrary to the calling of her soul. Contrary to what would make her soul sing.

The Kerry I am today is living the life that resulted from the decisions of the younger Kerry who needed approval and love so badly. I am living the life that resulted from the younger Kerry who didn't even consider what she wanted, what mattered to her.

She just walked along the path that was laid by the people she thought she could get love and approval from.

I was shocked to the core when I realized this. It was such a huge, albeit painful, realization. It reverberated within me for hours.

Have I forgiven that Kerry yet? No. But I'm thinking about her. And I want to forgive her.

Something has been happening to me during this pandemic season. It is like every single blinder has been ripped off my eyes. I can see clearly now. I see all the connections, all the reasons, all the history that made my life what it is today.

For many years, I thought I had a pretty good life. I thought I had enough. I thought I should just shut up and be grateful for what I have. The people I love most made it clear that this was exactly what I should do. Shut up. Be grateful. They made it clear that my wanting more was wrong. That I was wrong for wanting anything at all. That my emotions and needs and desires were unimportant.

I accepted that for many, many years. Lately, though, my soul has been calling to me. It's getting louder and louder, And, you know what it's saying? "You deserve all the things you dream of. You deserve the life you dream of. You deserve to be surrounded by people who love you and respect you and who want to transform alongside you."

I've never really had that, to be honest. The younger Kerry didn't think she deserved that. The Kerry I am today is just beginning to consider this. I created the life I thought I deserved. I created the relationships I thought I deserved. It was all my doing. I had nobody else to blame. I knew that. It makes it so hard to accept and even harder to forgive myself.

I am thinking of that earlier Kerry, the one who didn't think she deserved all of the things she dreamed of. Who allowed things that should never have happened to happen. Who accepted just about anything in her pursuit of love and approval. I see her now. I am starting to understand her.

I don't respect the younger Kerry though. I don't love her. I certainly don't forgive her. As I sit here, I imagine her in my mind's eye. I know I must forgive her. It won't be easy, but I know this is a massive block I have inside of me. It is a remnant of my past that holds me, keeps me in regret, keeps me in a victim mode. I am ready to release it. I will work to release it, to surrender, to forgive. To set the younger Kerry free. To release the charge and set myself free.

During the call, someone said that this forgiveness work is not for the faint of heart. In this moment, that sentence resonates within me. Not for the faint of heart indeed. As I write this book, I'm still working on forgiving myself. I know it is possible.

It's one of the greatest gifts
you can give yourself, to forgive.
Forgive everybody.
—Maya Angelou

*That perfect day,
that magic moment
that we're all waiting for,
is right now.*

—Kevin Griffin

CHAPTER 7

CREATIVE VISUALIZATION: PLAN YOUR PERFECT DAY, PERFECT LIFE, PERFECT YOU

*Not how long, but how well you
have lived is the main thing.*
—Seneca

MY PERFECT DAY

I never thought much about planning my perfect day until I started doing
the 6 Phase Meditation by Vishen Lakhiani. In it, he asks you to look
three years out into the future and to visualize that. Next, he asks you to
plan your perfect day with the idea of your ideal future in mind. What are
the things you would need to do today to make that happen? That question

clarified so much for me. I made that connection between my big hopes and dreams and my daily choices. I did that meditation for a very long time, and I still revisit it when I need some inspiration. It has been a game changer for me as I construct the life of my dreams. Each day is my life in miniature; I want to make it the best possible day I can. That's the power of planning your perfect day.

Every single thing you see around you was first created in somebody's mind. All that you see was first a thought in someone's mind which they took action on bringing the idea into physical form. All things are created this way. It starts with an idea, a thought, a vision. This primes our brain to look for what we need in order to bring the vision into physical form. By practicing creative visualization, we are harnessing the power of creation. We are bringing the unseen into the seen.

For many years, visualization was regarded as new age mumbo jumbo, however, in recent years, research has shown that visualization truly works. Yes, there is a scientific basis for visualization. A neuroscience-based research paper by the International Coaching Academy, stated that, "if you exercise an idea over and over [in your mind], your brain will begin to respond as though the idea was a real object in the world." The paper goes on to say that the thalamus makes no distinction between what you're thinking and what is actually happening. The brain does not distinguish between inner and outer realities. This means that if you think about something for a long enough time, it will seem real to the brain. The brain then begins to work with the idea, making it more familiar, more attainable. This, in turn, motivates the person to take action in the world so that they can create what was, until then, just a vision, just a dream. Creative visualization quite literally primes the brain for action.

The thalamus is a structure in the brain located just above the brainstem between the cerebral cortex and the midbrain. It is a small structure but it has extensive nerve connections which relays motor and sensory signals. The thalamus regulates consciousness and alertness so it quite literally creates reality, your reality. The thalamus is where you rehearse things so that when it's time to take action, you're ready. The thalamus is where the process of thinking about what you want to create in reality occurs. It is where 98 percent of all sensory input for perception is relayed. Think of it as a notepad for perception and planning.

For many years, it was believed that the thalamus simply served as a relay station from the sense organs to the cerebral cortex, a messaging center of sorts. However, in recent years, this idea has been challenged. A fascinating article by the Human Neuroimaging Institute of Neurology at the University College in London titled, "The Thalamus as a Blackboard for Perception and Planning" suggests that the traditional belief that the thalamus is simply a relay station vastly underestimates it's true function. "Recent studies suggest thalamic involvement in a very wide range of cognitive functions, including perception, attention (Saalman and Kastner, 2014; Wimmer et al., 2015; Schmitt et al., 2017), memory (Dumont and Aggleton, 2013; Warburton, 2018), task engagement (Marton et al., 2018), learning, motor control (Ouhaz et al., 2018), and executive decision-making (Do Monte et al., 2015)." Exciting, right?

The most amazing thing of all is that the brain quite literally constructs our reality. Our sense organs like our eyes, ears, nose, and skin take in information from the world around us and then use this information to create a picture of reality. It seems like what you are seeing is true reality but remember, everything is actually happening inside your brain.

I know what you're thinking. You're thinking that what you see HAS TO be reality. I get it. I grappled with this concept for years. And then, one day, I got it. Everything around me is quite literally a construction my brain is creating based upon my senses. Everything happening out there in the world is processed in the dark vault of your brain. Let's look into this concept a bit deeper. Come along with me on a brief journey through the amazing powers of our brain. Don't worry, I will keep it simple and accessible. No science degree necessary.

The brain's main purpose is to protect you, to keep you alive. In order to do that, we scan our surroundings constantly, using our senses to assess whether our surroundings are safe, whether we are safe. Our senses of sight, hearing, touch, and smell help us to bring information to our brain and then the brain assembles a picture of the surroundings we are in. Since the brain cannot process everything that is going on around it, the brain filters out information at times. At other times, the brain will actually fill in missing information. So there is always some information that we are not taking in, there is always some information that we are utterly ignoring, and then there are times when we fill in information based on the past.

There were a series of studies done that illustrated how little we actually take in from our surroundings. In the experiments, participants were asked to watch a video of people throwing a ball around and to count the number of times the ball was thrown. As this was happening, a man in a gorilla suit walked directly into the middle of the screen, banged on his chest for nine seconds and then walked off. Incredibly, half of the participants did not see the man in the gorilla suit. This illustrates how our brain constructs our beliefs and our experience.

The good news is that since everything is happening inside your brain, you can create any reality you want. You can visualize, envision, imagine your life, and your brain will believe it. Even more important, it will help to create the opportunities to act on your vision. Athletes have known this for years. Elite athletes going back decades have used this to imagine themselves performing their sport and doing it with ease and grace.

Bruce Jenner, who won the decathlon in 1976 practiced visualization for four years in order to win the gold. It is an amazing story, actually, and one we can all learn from. You see, Bruce Jenner lost the decathlon in Munich in 1972 but instead of crushing him, this loss ignited him to take massive action. He said that the moment he lost, he made the absolute decision to win in 1976. He made the decision to dedicate himself to training and to let nothing stop him. And that is exactly what happened. He spent the next four years in a training program he designed for himself. He worked tirelessly, day after day, honing his body, preparing himself for the events.

Not only did he do the things he needed to do physically in order to win, he also imagined himself victorious, standing on the victor's platform with the gold medal draped around his neck. Each night, he would lie in his bed imagining himself going through each event, executing the moves perfectly. He did this every single night. His final step was to alter a picture of the Munich gold medal winner standing on the podium with the gold medal. He replaced the winner's face with his own face. He won the mental game first. Bruce Jenner said that he won the medal in his mind first and went to the Olympics in Montreal to simply pick up the medal he had already one. Powerful, right?

There has been a lot of interest in learning how to integrate physical training with mental training. In a fascinating Soviet-funded program involving world-class athletes, the athletes were separated into four four groups. The first group did only physical training while the second group did 75 percent physical training and 25 percent mental training. The third group did 50 percent physical and 50 percent mental training while the fourth group did 25 percent physical training and 75percent mental training. The four groups were compared before the 1980 Winter Games in Lake Placid and the results were startling. The athletes in group four who did only 25 percent physical training and 75 percent mental training had greater improvements than the third group that did equal parts physical and mental training. In a shocking twist, the first group that had done the most physical training, 100 percent physical training to be exact, had the least improvement in performance. This indicates that mental training is essential.

Mental training has now become an integral part of professional athletic training practices. Michael Jordan, arguably the best basketball player of all time, the original GOAT, practiced visualization before every single game as did the amazing Kobe Bryant. They both worked with George Mumford who is the "Mindfulness Meditation Coach." Mumford also worked with Shaquille O'Neale and Phil Jackson. Mumford himself overcame addiction by applying positive thinking, and it must have worked pretty well for him considering he worked with three of the all-time basketball greats.

If that doesn't convince you, then maybe this will, Tom Brady started using visualization and mindfulness practices in his college days. He went on to work with a health and fitness coach named Alex Guerrero who overhauled Tom's diet and trained him in the mental aspects of the game. Tom said, "To me, football is so much about mental toughness." With five Super Bowl wins, four Super Bowl MVPs, and two League MVPs, it's pretty hard to argue with Brady about pretty much anything at this point.

A discussion on athletes and visualization would not be complete without talking about the most decorated Olympian of all time. With a record 28 medals, Michael Phelps captured the hearts and minds of the world. Who wasn't swept away when Phelps won an astonishing eight gold medals at the 2008 Beijing Olympics? And how did he do it? With visualization. Michael Phelps used visualization to not only imagine his wins, he also used visualization to imagine what he would do if something went wrong. He mentally rehearsed everything before his races. If it worked for him, then why not give it a chance? Let's visualize!

BENEFITS OF CREATIVE VISUALIZATION

Creative Visualization Improves:
- focus
- confidence
- trust
- resilience
- sense of peace
- autonomy over your life
- intentional living
- perspective
- creativity
- planning skills

Creative Visualization Reduces:
- stress

- anxiety
- overwhelm
- brain fog

THE EXERCISES

EXERCISE 1: VISUALIZE YOUR PERFECT DAY

The first exercise is a part of the 6 Phase Meditation by Vishen Lakhiani. The 6 Phase is a full 20-minute meditation that walks you through compassion, gratitude, forgiveness, visualizing your future, planning your perfect day, and a blessing. It is a great way to start your day if you have the time. As an extra credit project, you can try the 6 Phase during one of your Snooze Button Sessions, but you might just need to reset your alarm so it doesn't go off midway through the meditation. I will give you a gold star if you do the 6 Phase Meditation, however, if you don't have the time for the full practice, you can try just one piece of it, planning your perfect day.

Visualizing your perfect day is a great way to pre-plan and work out how your day will go. By going through your day from morning to night, imagining all the things you have to do and envisioning your day going right, you are setting yourself up for success. As you think about your day, you begin with the moment you get up and walk through the entire day. As you do so, you imagine the very best outcome for each segment of your day. You imagine the perfect breakfast with the most delicious food, the best commute to work, arriving at work and greeting your coworkers with joy, beginning your workday with all your work going smoothly and then continuing on through the perfect lunch with your ideal lunch partners and then back to work. Maybe you visualize some exercise and then through your dinner and evening activities, all the way back to the moment when you are where you started, snug in your bed. Thinking about your day like this is very enjoyable, and you can consider it a practice for the actual activities. A dry run of the day. Are you ready? Let's do it.

Go to kerryfishercoaching.com for the video resource for this exercise.

PRACTICE

- Hit your snooze button and sit up straight.
- Relax your body from head to toes.
- Begin to imagine your perfect day.
- Imagine what you will do once you get up and begin your day.
- What will you do? Will you work first? Exercise? Spend time with family? Eat breakfast? Sit with your lover and have some tea or coffee? Sit outside and listen to the bird's sing? It's your day; how will you begin it?
- Construct your perfect morning. Everything is going perfectly, all is well.
- Then what? What do you do for the late morning, early afternoon?
- Imagine you are productive, on target, on track, all is going as planned. Meetings are going the way you dream of; your work is getting done; you are interacting well with everyone you meet.
- Now imagine your lunch. It is the perfect lunch. Who will you eat with? What will you eat? Treat yourself well. Make it the best lunch you can imagine.
- Think about the afternoon now. What will you be doing, what activities, what work will you do? Who will you spend time with?
- Now it is dinner time. Who do you eat with? Where are you eating? What are you eating? Imagine it perfectly, down to the smallest detail.
- Imagine the end of your day, your evening. Will you relax, spend time with family or friends?
- Now imagine you are getting ready for bed. Prepare your house for slumber as you go room to room dimming the lights, creating some relaxing ambiance. Maybe you light some candles or

incense, put on some relaxing music. It's your night, let it go just as you would if it went perfectly.

- Now imagine you are back in your bed. You are reflecting back upon your perfect day, and you resolve to have another perfect day tomorrow.
- You go to sleep and have a very restful, relaxing, refreshing sleep.

All that we see or seem is but a dream within a dream.
—Edgar Allan Poe

EXERCISE 2: VISUALIZE YOUR DREAM LIFE IN THREE YEARS

This is a similar exercise to the one above where you imagine your perfect day but this time, you are constructing your ideal future life. You will envision out three years and go step-by-step, imagining the dream life you have always wanted to have. For this exercise, do not limit yourself at all. Allow yourself to go wild and dream your very biggest dreams. Tap into the child within you who had big hopes, big goals. Let your imagination soar.

You might be wondering why this is helpful. You might be tempted to dream up things you think you CAN accomplish. But that's not what you are doing here. You want to dream big in order to let your brain get to work helping you get to the ideal life you always hoped for. You are priming your brain for action, so you might as well allow yourself the luxury of shooting for your biggest dreams. The very biggest dreams you can imagine.

Go to kerryfishercoaching.com for the video resource for this exercise.

PRACTICE

- Hit your snooze button and sit up in bed.

- Do a quick head to toe relaxation. Take a deep breath in and a long, slow breath out.
- Imagine it is three years in the future. You are living your ideal life, the life of your wildest imagination.
- Begin by imagining what you look like. What are you wearing, what kind of shape are you in? Are you dressed impeccably? Are you fit and fabulous?
- Where do you live? What does your house look like? Imagine every detail from the furnishings to the room setup, to the location, to the property itself. Dream your perfect home.
- How are your relationships? Imagine all your loved ones there in your home, they are celebrating something. They are celebrating...wait, they are celebrating YOU and all your accomplishments. They are celebrating you having created an incredible life, complete with the gorgeous home they are all gathered in. Look around and take it all in. The lovely people, the delicious food, the smells, the sounds, the ambiance.
- Now, you imagine what career you have., Remember, this is your dream so allow yourself to create the career you have always dreamed of. Each day you go to work that you love, you are living your mission.
- Continue imagining this perfect life until the alarm goes off. If you need more time because you are having so much fun in your dream future, then hit the snooze button one more time and continue your imagining until all the details have been worked out.

Note: If you are really serious about creating your perfect life, you can take one more step in this exercise. Once the alarm rings once more, think about one step you can take today to move strongly in the direction of your dreams. Resolve to make that step today and then again tomorrow and every single day until you bring your dream life into reality. Don't go to bed tonight unless you take that one small step.

I have visualized my imagination so clearly and so consistently
that it has manifested itself into my reality.
—Conor McGregor

EXERCISE 3: JOURNAL YOUR PERFECT DAY OR DREAM FUTURE

We will talk about the benefits of journaling in a future chapter. For now, just grab a journal, a notebook, your computer, or a piece of paper and simply do either the perfect day exercise or the perfect future exercise but instead of visualizing it, you will write it down. This is a powerful practice because it is a visualization with all the benefits associated with that, but you end up with a written description of what you want to happen. This is great because you can read and reread it, further cementing it into your head. Try it. Hit the snooze and allow yourself to free write.

EXERCISE 4: VISUALIZE YOUR IDEAL SELF

The ideal self-visualization will help you to create a mind map of the future you, the future self that you want to become. This is very similar to the perfect day and dream life visualizations above. The Ideal Self Visualization will allow you to consider how you want to look physically, how you want your relationships to look, what career you want to have, what fun adventures you want to go on, what hobbies you want to incorporate. Just as you did above, please allow yourself to freely visualize the most expansive version of you. Don't hold back. Ok, hit that snooze button and let's get started.

Go to kerryfishercoaching.com for the video resource for this exercise.

Note: This exercise can also be done as a journaling exercise.

PRACTICE

- Sit up in bed or on a chair and take a deep breath in and a long, slow breath out.
- Imagine yourself three years in the future.
- What do you look like physically? Just as in the perfect life visualization, imagine yourself looking exactly as you want to look, wearing exactly what you want to wear and feeling like you really want to feel.
- As you think about this future you, imagine where you are. Are you living in an exotic locale or are you in your dream home? Allow yourself to dream big. Picture the location in as much detail as possible and imagine how it feels to be there.
- What activities do you do each day? Do you take adventures? Do you travel? Do you relax and sit in nature simply enjoying your life? Imagine your day.
- Imagine now what you do for a living, what career you have? Let this be your dream career, work that fills you up and makes you feel like you are living on purpose, living your mission.
- Finally, you envision your relationships. Imagine relationships so deep and soulful that they make you feel amazing. Friendships and family relationships so deep and meaningful that they fill you with peace and joy. You are surrounded by people who inspire you, hold you accountable, encourage you and support you in all ways. And you do the same for them. Relationships where you each want the best for the other. Imagine relationships like that! Wow.
- As you wrap up your visualization, take a mental snapshot of this ideal you, this ideal self and resolve to move towards that vision each day.
- As a final step, you can get up and do one thing to move you strongly in the direction of your ideal self. Do that today, tomor-

row, and every day and before you know it, you will become that person you dreamed of becoming.

Visualization is daydreaming with a purpose.
—Robert Foster Bennett

EXERCISE 5: CREATIVE VISUALIZATION FOR EVERY ACTIVITY

The beauty of having learned the above visualization exercises is that you can now apply this technique to any event or activity or meeting that you have. You can visualize that important presentation from start to finish, with every aspect going perfectly. Or if you have an important event or holiday you are planning, you can envision it all going beautifully with great food, great company, and a great time had by all. Anything that you have to do can be visualized in advance. Think of it like a warm up for the actual event. It will help things go smoothly and might even release some of the anxiety and stress that often accompanies important activities in your life.

PRACTICE

- Begin by sitting up straight with your chin parallel to the floor. Breathe in deeply and then let out a long, slow exhale.
- Do the head-to-toe relaxation exercise, moving from the top of your head all the way down to your feet, relaxing each part of your body in turn.
- Bring to mind a future event, meeting, vacation, or activity you have coming up.

- Allow yourself to picture the entire event from beginning to end, making sure that in your creative visualization, everything flows perfectly.
- Continue going through the event step by step, envisioning all the details that you can.
- Feel the excitement, happiness, and joy you feel as you think about this event going so smoothly.
- Give the feeling a color and imagine the scene in your mind surrounded by that color.
- Expand the emotion more and more, allowing the color to become as vivid as you can.
- Think the words, "And so it is, it is so."
- Release the picture in your mind, knowing it will all go as you imagined it would.
- Gently open your eyes and journal any notes you may have or observations from the visualization.

All that we see or seem is but a dream within a dream.
—Edgar Allan Poe

How to Bring Creative Visualization into Your Day

Creative Visualization is a great practice to begin your day but it is also a great way to end your day. When you get into bed at night, go through your day, and think about the day. What did you learn? Who did you help? You might do what Benjamin Franklin did each night and think about what you could improve. Simply think about something that did not go as planned during your day and then consider how you could do it better next time. Visualize the situation once again but this time, with the outcome that you prefer to have. This way, the next time a situation like this occurs, you are ready and know how you want to act. The great thing about this technique is that instead of beating yourself up over your missteps and mistakes, you use those moments when you weren't at your best as teaching moments. You use them as a training ground for your future behavior.

REFLECT

1. What comes up for you as you do your visualizations? Are you freely able to visualize or are you having some resistance?
2. Write down some of the ideas you had as you went through your creative visualization practice. Were there themes that were repeated or challenges that popped up? Write them down.
3. When you imagined your dream life and the version of you that you imagine, how did that make you feel? Do you feel like you can step into this vision or does it seem out of reach? Do some journaling about this.
4. If you have doubt that you can really create the visions that you are imagining, write down why you think this, what is stopping you? Do you have some old beliefs that need to be rewritten? Do that now.
5. Sit quietly and reflect on what it would be like if it was three years in the future and all your wildest dreams have come true. Write about the emotions that come up for you as you imagine this. Allow yourself to truly feel all the emotions, letting them wash over you. Journal about how it feels in your body to have the life you dream about.

DREAM IT, BELIEVE IT, ACHIEVE IT

In my childhood days as a competitive gymnast, I was lucky to have an incredible coach named Diane. Diane was a woman way ahead of her time. She was interested in health and wellness, meditation and mindful-

ness, breathwork and visualization long before these things were commonly discussed. Our team always performed very well during our competitions. Diane had a high standard, and we trained hard but looking back, I realized that Diane was using a secret weapon that the other coaches weren't using way back then. You see, Diane was teaching us creative visualization, having us visualize each and every one of our routines every single day. She told us that the first thing when we wake up and the last thing before we fall asleep each night, we should run through our routines and imagine them going perfectly. She explained how we should imagine every single move we make, every single flip, every single dance move, even the final smile at the judges at the end of the routine. I did this every single night for all the years I competed, and I am sure that it is what made all the difference to my performance and to the team's success.

Diane had one more trick up her sleeve though. During the competitions, you could see our entire team sitting on the sidelines stretching, but what you couldn't see was that we were each mentally going through the next routine we were slated to compete in. We didn't speak much during our competitions. When we weren't cheering on our teammates, we were silently preparing in our minds, executing the routine perfectly in our heads. Many times, by the time I went up to compete, I had zero nervousness. I felt like I had done the routine so many times that one more time was no big deal. And guess what? I had done the routine many times, in my head. Performing it in reality felt easy because by the time I got up there, I had primed myself for action.

That is the power of creative visualization, and it is something I have carried through my life. It has helped me through many, many difficult situations and many joyous ones as well. In a very real way, when I use creative visualization, I am teaching myself how to feel, how to act. If I can do it, you can do it. I urge you to bring this practice into your life. Imagine what it could do! I'm serious. Go ahead. Imagine!

> *Visualizing is daydreaming with a purpose.*
> —Bo Bennett

Think before you speak.
Read before you think.

—FRAN LEBOWITZ

CHAPTER 8

INSPIRING WORDS: UPLIFTING LITERATURE, PODCASTS, AND CONTENT

The best books are those that tell you what you know already.
—George Orwell

I *was lucky enough to have a mother who always encouraged my read-ing. Even more important than that, my mother always modeled good habits by reading incessantly. When I was about ten years old, I found my mother's collection of Agatha Christie books. I knew I probably wasn't supposed to read them, so I would take one, sneak away and read the book and then swap it for the next book when I was done. I loved those books.*

One day, my mother walked into my room while I was reading, and I jumped about a mile in the air because she had caught me red handed reading her book. I quickly threw the book down, so she couldn't see it. My mom was very cool, calm, and collected. She didn't comment on the book; she just told me I needed to clean up my room. As she was walking out of the room, she turned back to me and said, "Kerry, you are old enough to read anything you want. You can read any book in the house." And without another word, she left. I was relieved. I was happy that I didn't get in trouble but even more importantly, now I could read whatever I wanted without hiding. I always think about that simple comment she made, and I am grateful to have a mom who was so open minded and so interested in nurturing my love of reading.

There was another incident that locked in my love of reading and my love for my mother. Every week, my mom would bring me to the library to get books. I loved it. I basically started at one end of the children's section and continued on until I had read all the books in that part of the library. I was getting bored with the "baby" books so one day, I crept over to the other side of the library where the adult books were, and I started perusing the shelves. One of the librarians came up to me and told me to go back to the kid's section. All of a sudden, my mom appeared and told the librarian that I had her permission to read any book in the library I wanted.

That was the day the entire world of literature opened up to me. I didn't let the opportunity slip away. I read it all—science fiction, history, autobiographies, romance, psychology, philosophy, and spirituality. My curiosity knew no bounds. I still read like that. Reading is something that has remained constant in my life, and it always will.

> *We become what we think about most of the time.*
> —Earl Nightingale

Lifelong learning is one of the best ways to ensure that you will maintain a healthy brain for all the days of your life. Reading (or listening to) amazing books, listening to podcasts, and finding content that inspires you can literally change your brain. A growing body of research using

MRI scans shows that complex networks of circuits in the brain get stronger as you improve your reading ability. It has been shown the more often you read, the better your brain connectivity becomes.

Here is something even more fascinating. Reading fiction actually improves our empathy, enabling us to better understand other people's feelings. Levels of empathy actually increase with long term reading.

Reading also has a measurable effect on stress levels in the body. Simply reading for a few minutes per day lowers heart rate and blood pressure. A 2013 study found that people who use their brains for stimulating activities like reading, learning, and doing crossword puzzles are much less likely to develop some of the lesions that are found in the brains of people who develop Alzheimers and dementia.

If you aren't interested in reading, you can get the same content by listening to audio books. Audio books are a great way to catch up on some of the books you have been meaning to read and the best thing about audio books is that you can listen to them at fast speed. Try your audio book at 1 ½ speed or double speed. Listening at faster speeds often makes you pay closer attention than you would if you listened at regular speed so give this a try. Challenge yourself by experimenting with how fast you can listen without losing the ability to follow the plot. The coolest thing about this is that one short snooze session can get you double the listening if you go to a faster speed. Try it!

You don't just have to turn to books for your inspiring content. We are lucky that we live in a time when there are countless podcasts, online courses, and short instructional videos that we can access, usually free of charge. Ask some of your friends what podcasts they listen to or browse podcasts and see what grabs your attention. Make sure you pick the podcast, course, or video you want to listen to the night before you begin this practice, so you don't spend the entire Snooze Button Session searching for the perfect material. Be ready with it and have it cued up the night before. Then when the alarm rings in the morning, you'll be ready.

BENEFITS OF INSPIRING WORDS

Inspiring Words Improve:
- brain function
- vocabulary and comprehension
- memory
- focus
- concentration
- analytical thinking
- ability to empathize/connect with others
- sleep

Inspiring Words Reduce:
- stress
- depression
- cognitive decline
- mental fog
- blood pressure
- heart rate

THE EXERCISES

EXERCISE 1: READING

Here's a fun fact. *The Tale of Genji* is often called the world's first novel. It was written 1,000 years ago by a woman named Murasaki Shikibu. The book, a 54-chapter story of seduction, is the tale of 11th century Japan. Although this book is billed as the world's first novel, there were other long tales of prose before this book, dating back about 2,000 years. Reading connects you to this long history of readers before you. Pretty amazing, isn't it?

You can read books on a variety of topics ranging from fiction to science fiction to religion to spirituality to personal transformation to business. These are just a few of the many genres you can choose from. If you really want to get inspired, read autobiographies. You will learn that every story is powerful, every story is a true hero's journey.

To get you started, here are a few of my all-time favorite authors: Dan Millman, Paulo Coelho, Don Miguel Ruis, Carlos Castaneda, Og Mandino, Wayne Dyer, Hermann Hesse, The Dalai Lama, Ayn Rand, Nassim Nicholas Taleb, Kurt Vonnegut, Jordan Peterson and Dale Carnegie.

The best memoir that I have ever read is *Will* by Will Smith. I got it in the mail, sat down and didn't get back up until I finished the book. Yes, it's that good. It's a read-it-in-one-sitting book. Some other incredible autobiographies and biographies: *Jobs* by Walter Isaason, *Is the Noise in My Head Bothering You* by Steven Tyler, *The Diary of a Young Girl* by Anne Frank, *Becoming* by Michelle Obama, *Long Walk to Freedom* by Nelson Mandela, *When Breath Becomes Air* by Paul Kalanithi, *Open* by Andre Agassi and *Autobiography of a Yogi* by Paramahansa Yogananda.

Here is a partial listing of some of my all-time favorite books: *The Way of the Peaceful Warrior* by Dan Milllman, *The Alchemist* by Paulo Coelho, *The Four Agreements* by Don Miguel Ruiz, *Journey to Ixtlan* by Carlos Castaneda, *Think and Grow Rich* by Napoleon Hill, *Atlas Shrugged* by Ayn Rand, *Inner Engineering* by Sadghuru and *Cosmos* by Carl Sagan.

Try one of the above books, ask a friend for a good book suggestion or scroll through Amazon and order a book that piques your interest. Read a few pages or a few chapters if you have the time. Begin your day by filling your mind and spirit with the words of the masters. Let it be a balm to your soul. As you read, allow yourself to feel the connection between you and the author and all the other people who ever read that book. Maybe, just maybe, you even feel the golden thread connecting you to the people who read that very first novel, *The Tale of the Genji*, over a thousand years ago.

Pro Tip: Keep your book next to your bed, right next to your alarm clock, so you can hit the snooze and grab the book. Make sure to pick the book out the night before, so you are ready. Once you get into this habit, you can keep the book in the bedside drawer but until the habit is installed, place the book directly next to your alarm clock. Remember to make these techniques easy, so you can build in success.

> *To learn to read is to light a fire;*
> *every syllable that is spelled out is a spark.*
> —Victor Hugo

EXERCISE 2: PODCASTS AND UPLIFTING CONTENT

We often think that we are living in a time of great upheaval and chaos and that things have never been worse. In fact, things have never been better for humans. We live in a world where we have, in the form of our cellphones, all the world's knowledge at our fingertips. We can access esoteric information that was once reserved for only the highest echelon of spiritual seekers. There are endless videos and classes and informational podcasts that we can access. It is truly amazing when you think about it.

You can find a lot of this content for free by searching YouTube or doing a quick computer search. You can also scroll through the huge variety of podcasts that are out there. You will find that there is a podcast on any and every topic you can imagine. As you search for content, let your curiosity be your guide. Experiment with different podcasters, different podcast lengths, and different topics.

How to Bring Inspiring Words into Your Day

Now that you are beginning your day with inspiring words, why not take the next step and listen to inspiring content throughout the day?

There are many times during the day that you can claw back your time by choosing to listen to something educational instead of spending time on meaningless tasks. For instance, when you go on social media, you might get sucked in and before you know it, an hour or more has passed and all you have to show for it is that you now know that your friend loves to drink fancy cappuccino. Instead of getting lost in social media, set a timer for five minutes before you go on social media and when the timer goes off, switch to a podcast, audio book or an informational video.

Another fantastic time to listen to content is when you are in the car. If you commute, you can dedicate one or both ways of the commute to learning. Get this queued up and ready before you drive and make sure the content is long enough so you don't have to fumble with your phone as you drive. Long car rides when you are taking a trip is another great time to listen. This is a perfect time to listen to audio books since they go from chapter to chapter without you having to do anything. The great thing about listening during your travels is that if you get stuck in traffic, it won't even bother you because you can just listen to more of your book! It might change everything about your feelings about commuting.

Since you are beginning your day with uplifting content, why not end your day that way as well? Bookending your day with reading is such a nourishing practice you can add to your day. The best part of this is that you can jump into bed, read your book all snug and cozy and then, as you become drowsy, simply put the book on the nightstand next to you, turn off the light and go to sleep. Then, when you wake up, your book is there, ready to go. Easy as can be!

Find time throughout your day to nourish your mind with the words of the world's masters. It is absolutely incredible that we have the opportunity to read or listen to the words of the wise men and women who came before us and who knows? All that reading and listening might inspire you to get creative. You never know. As a lifelong reader, I want to encourage you to try to add daily reading to your life. Books have been my solace through the good times and the bad, the happy times and the sad. It is my wish that they become that for you as well.

When we fill our brains with positive messages, we are training our brain. And who knows, the next time you get stuck in traffic or you are confronted with some minor annoyance, you might just be influenced enough to choose to see the situation differently. Maybe, just maybe, you choose not to get angry or upset or stressed out. Instead, you might simply choose to take that extra time and listen to some music or relax in the car, or you could even decide to take that time to listen to *more* uplifting content to develop a deeper level of understanding. This, my friends, is when your life begins to change at a level that is actually creating a more comfortable, happy, and even meaningful experience throughout your normal days.

By intentionally selecting the positive input through positive or uplifting literature, podcasts, and other content, we are rewiring our brains, teaching ourselves to focus on the positive, and learning new things to nourish our brain. It's a total win-win-win. Yes, that's a thing.

Remember, you have control over how you choose to spend your life. Choose wisely.

> *Whatever we plant in our subconscious mind and nourish*
> *with repetition and emotion will one day become a reality.*
> —Earl Nightingale

REFLECT

1. What could you read or listen to during your Snooze Button Session that will make you happy and set you up for an incredible day?
2. Sit down and make a list of all the things you are interested in. Don't hold back, write anything and everything that pops into your mind without censoring yourself. Pick one thing from the list and study this every day for a week. At the end of the week, decide if you want to keep studying this topic or you want to learn about something else on your list.

3. Make a list of all the times during the day when you find that you are wasting time. Make a list of the activities that you are doing that are a waste of your time. Look at the list and pick one time of day or one activity that you will replace with reading or listening to content that educates you.

4. Make a list of all the interests and hobbies you had as a child and in your young adulthood. Ask friends and family what they remember about what you were interested in. Then, pick one thing and incorporate that back into your life.

5. Find the times in your day that you can "claw back" your time and replace it with uplifting content. Challenge yourself here.

Nourish the mind like you would your body.
The mind cannot survive on junk food.
—Jim Rohn

Writing in a journal reminds you of your goals and of your learning in life. It offers a place where you can hold a deliberate, thoughtful conversation with yourself.

—ROBIN SHARMA

CHAPTER 9

JOURNALING

I don't journal to be productive.
I don't do it to find great ideas or to put down prose I can later publish.
The pages aren't intended for anyone but me.
It's the most cost-effective therapy I've ever found.
—Tim Ferriss

Journaling is a great way to process your emotions, to gain clarity, and to keep a record of what is happening in your life. Journaling provides a space for you to ponder how you really feel about things as well as a place to explore your feelings more deeply. Traditionally, people would purchase a journal and then write in it, however, these days, there are many different ways you can record your thoughts. You can use a beautiful journal dedicated to your daily journaling practice, or you can create a document or use your phone to record an audio journal. Some people even enjoy making video journals, simply putting on the video on their phone and talking away. It doesn't really matter how you journal, it just matters that you actually journal.

Journaling has proven mental and physical health benefits. The emerging science shows journaling can reduce depression and anxiety, help you process uncomfortable emotions, boost immune function and improve your memory. A Stice, Burton, Bearman, and Rohde study done in 2006 showed that journal writing reduces overall levels of depression, oftentimes showing the same effectiveness as therapy.

A study done at UCLA measured brain activity during journaling therapy and found that the experience of trauma was greatly reduced by the act of writing. According to Stice, Burton, Bearman, and Rohde, journaling was as effective as cognitive behavioral therapy for reducing depression in high-risk adolescents.

Another study broke participants into two groups with one group writing about their deepest emotions and the other group simply journaling about their day. The group who wrote about their emotions used fewer brain resources on tasks performed after the writing, showing that expressive writing is helpful in preparing the mind for higher performance on future activities.

As we can see, journaling is great for processing difficult emotions and clearing the mind. Journaling is also great for figuring out where you are now and where you want to go. This is why journaling is known as a keystone habit. A keystone habit is a habit that produces a ripple effect where the one positive change, journaling, can lead to many other positive changes in other areas of your life. So are you ready? Let's journal.

Documenting details of your everyday life
becomes a celebration of who you are.
—Carolyn V. Hamilton

MY JOURNALING PRACTICE BY DANI GLASSER

I have always loved to write, but there is something about journaling that calms and centers me. I prefer to do it in the morning, pen in one hand, a hot cup of tea near the other. I listen to the sound of the pen upon paper as I write the words, watching the ink flow. It is a sensory experience on the physical level, and yet a spiritual and intellectual one as well as I convert my thoughts into words on a page. It's a bit like meditation in many ways.

For me, journaling has evolved over the years. It started out just keeping track of my life, venting about people in my life, pouring out my vulnerabilities, keeping notes and quotes. Eventually, it has become a tool to explore who I am as a person, process emotions, deconstruct goals, and work through challenges. It is a place to ask questions, and seek out answers. It brings a sense of awareness.

As I journal, I can feel the stress decrease as I become grounded by the physical experience. I am giving myself space to process, deconstruct, and work through things. It is so much more than a space to plop down words. It is therapeutic, as I am giving myself the time and space to connect with myself. It is the space to record what I hear within me, to know my thoughts and desires, and gain clarity in my life and mind.

BENEFITS OF JOURNALING

Journaling Improves:
- immune system function
- cognitive function
- memory
- focus
- creativity
- healthy emotional management
- self-awareness

Journaling Reduces:
- stress
- symptoms of depression

- overwhelm
- unorganized/Sporadic thinking

A pen to paper
Creating words from my thoughts.
Sensory solace.
—Dani Glasser

THE EXERCISES

EXERCISE 1: BRAIN DUMP

This is a great exercise to start with. You can use a piece of paper for this one or a note on your phone. You will simply hit the snooze button and then write down every single thing you have to do. Yes, everything. Write everything, big and small, that you have to accomplish. By getting the thoughts out of your head and onto the paper, you free up your mind to think about more important things. This is a simple yet powerful exercise.

PRACTICE

- Hit your snooze button, grab your journal and pen and begin.
- Here are some ideas:
- Write down everything that is on your mind.
- Write the things you have to do that day.
- Write your goals.
- Write what you have to do in the future.
- Write your petty annoyances you have.
- Write a list of people who annoyed you.
- Write a list of all the things you are grateful for.
- Write all of the errands you need to do.

- Write what hopes and dreams you have for your career, yourself, your kids.
- Write a list of the adventures you want to have,

EXERCISE 2: DREAM JOURNAL

Keeping a dream journal is a really interesting way to start understanding yourself better. Keep your journal directly next to your bed and as soon as you hit your snooze button, begin to write down everything you can remember from your dreams. It is essential that you write as quickly as you can, before your dreams fly back away into dreamland. When you first start to keep track of your dreams, you may find that you can't remember much but keep with it. As the days pass, you will notice that you remember more and more from your dreams. Think of this as a muscle you are training. You will get better with practice.

As you continue keeping a dream journal, see if you can spot patterns within your dreams. Are you going to the same location in your dreams each time? Are you seeing the same people? Perhaps you are participating in the same activities in your dreams. Once you spot patterns, think about what it might mean. Perhaps your subconscious is telling you something.

PRACTICE

- As soon as the alarm rings, grab your journal and start to write.
- Try to have as little time as possible between opening your eyes and writing down your dreams.
- Don't think, just write.
- Keep doing this for at least a month in order to increase your recall.
- **Pro Tip**: before you go to bed each evening, put your journal and pen right next to your alarm. As you fall asleep, remind yourself that you will remember your dreams, This will set you up for success.

EXERCISE 3: JOURNALING

A very nice way to begin your day. Simply grab your journal and begin to write. Allow your thoughts to flow freely; do not censor yourself. Breathe slowly and deeply to stay in a relaxed state as you let the thoughts flow from your mind straight down to the paper. You can do this for one Snooze Button Session or more. Keep writing until you have nothing left to write. If you have time, you can read what you wrote or perhaps you want to read it at night before bed. Another option is waiting until the end of the week and then reading the entire week's journal entries. This is a great way to get to know yourself. When you re-read your words, notice if you have any themes that arise. Notice the tone of your writing...are you happy, sad, complaining, grateful? Learn about who you are and how you feel by this simple act of journaling.

> You must remember that your story matters.
> What you write has the power to save a life,
> sometimes that life is your own.
> —Stalina Goodwin

EXERCISE 4: GRATITUDE JOURNAL

Congratulations, you already know this one from the gratitude chapter! Here's the chance to revisit it if you liked it or to try it for the first time if you didn't try it for your gratitude week. Simple yet effective—you hit your snooze button, pick up your gratitude journal and list ten things that you are grateful for. If you want to go even further, write ten things that you are grateful for about yourself, ten things you are grateful for about your life, and ten things that you are grateful for about your career.

Make this a regular practice. Periodically review your gratitude journal to remind yourself that you have so many things to be grateful for. If you are going through a difficult time in life, remember that you can always grab your gratitude journal and read it just like I did that first day of the pandemic. It will remind you that as long as you have breath in your body, there is something to be grateful for.

JOURNALING TOPICS

- Your Hopes and Dreams
- Wins You Have Had
- Challenges You Are Facing
- Family Journal
- Things You Are Happy About
- Things that You Are Not Happy About
- Work life, home life, family life, kids, spouse, yourself
- Am I Living My True Purpose?
- Your Health
- Your Financial Situation
- What I Have Learned This Week
- Who Did I Help This Week?
- The Words I Want to Live by Are...
- Make a List of the People Who Love You
- Make a List of the People You Love
- What Do I Love About My Life?

HOW TO BRING JOURNALING INTO YOUR DAY

The easiest way to bring journaling into your day is by having a note or document on your phone where you can quickly jot down anything that comes to mind, things you learn, aha moments. You can also use the record feature on your phone to do this. Simply grab your phone, press record, and then say what you have to say. Listen back to this when you have the chance. You might learn something new about yourself.

You can add journaling in as a nighttime routine as well, right before bed. You could write down what you did that day, wins, challenges. You could reflect on the great things you accomplished, the people you helped. Another great nighttime ritual is to write down anything beautiful you witnessed that day. Whether it is a butterfly or a beautiful flower, a mother with her baby, a bird flying by or simply the smile of a stranger, write it down. When we begin to notice the beauty that we see around us, the world around us begins to be even more beautiful.

REFLECT

1. How does it feel when you journal?
2. How do you feel when you read the journal back to yourself?
3. What are the common themes that come up when you journal?
4. What is the tone of your journaling? Take note of predominant emotions that crop up again and again.
5. Do you notice any changes in the rest of your day when you begin the day by journaling?

DREAMS OF FLYING

When I was a child, I had very vivid dreams. Dreams of flying up high into the universe and beyond and dreams of fantastical animals. I had dreams that were happy, sad, and everything in between. They were technicolor dreams, and they were wonderful. In my dreams, I could do anything, be anything; I was invincible, and it was incredible.

As I got older, I realized I no longer dreamed so vividly. Or if I did, I certainly didn't remember my dreams.

I started to write down my dreams each morning and a funny thing happened. I realized I was still dreaming, but my dreams were not so vivid and, in my flying dreams, I stayed close to the ground. As the days went on, and I continued to write my dreams down each morning, I noticed that my dreams were getting more and more colorful, more and more vivid. It's so lovely to watch this happening. In my dreams, I'm still flying close to the ground, but I'm working on that too. Soon I will be flying as high as my dream imagination allows me to. To the universe and beyond!

> *A journal is your completely unaltered voice.*
> —Lucy Dacus

Intimacy transcends the physical. It is a feeling of closeness that isn't about proximity but of belonging. It is a beautiful emotional space in which two become one.

—STEVE MARABOLI

CHAPTER 10

CONNECTION: INTIMACY, TOUCH, HUG, AND MASSAGE

Communication is merely an exchange of information,
but connection is an exchange of our humanity.
—Sean Stephenson

THE HUG

I *remember the first time I ever saw people give each other true, loving hugs in public. I was taking a yoga class, and we were in the lobby before class. I saw two yoga teachers see each other, light up, and then run over to hug one another. As I watched them, they hugged and hugged and hugged. Honestly, it seemed odd to me at the time, unnaturally long.*

It stuck in my head, though, and definitely made an impression on me. Years later, when I became a yoga teacher, I walked into a yoga studio and saw an old friend. We ran towards one another and hugged and hugged and hugged. I had a flashback to that day years before, and I laughed to myself. I finally understood how nice a long, loving hug really was. If we ever meet, I'll show you what I mean. I have one hug reserved just for you.

The importance and value of human connection cannot be overstated. Our earliest ancestors worked together as a group; they were defined by their tribe. The tribe was what allowed our distant ancestors to survive and thrive in very harsh environments. The tribe created customs and rituals which shaped the way they lived. They were defined by the customs and rituals they shared—the way they worshipped, and by the things they had in common rather than the things that made them different. They lived and worked together for the sake of the whole. They stood together, stronger because of the group. The group kept everyone safe, helped everyone procure food, water, and shelter. The group helped keep everyone alive.

In modern times, we have moved away from this close-knit type of living. We are living in a time where we are more disconnected from one another than ever before. Although technology has brought us together in many ways, it has also divided us, leaving each of us alone, in our homes, behind a screen. This has led to a lack of physical human connection, which is very detrimental to our health. We are social beings; it's how we are wired.

Touch is one of the many ways we as humans connect. A study done in Sweden found that embracing children in distress has a soothing effect for them. Another series of studies conducted by Dutch researchers showed hugging could relieve a person's feelings of existential fear and remove self-doubt. These are just the tip of the iceberg when it comes to studies showing the important role that touch plays in our development, communication, personal relationships, and health. Massage is just one way we use touch intentionally in our society. Massage has been shown to decrease stress by lowering cortisol levels. Even more interesting, massage has been shown to increase the body's natural antidepressant and anti-pain chemical by releasing serotonin into the body. Isn't it amazing that something as simple as touching one another can cause our body to react in that way? Let's face it. When we hug and touch, we simply feel good. It's good for body, mind, and spirit.

When my kids were babies, I learned a silly little trick I had all but forgotten about until I was thinking about the importance of touch with my children. My husband and I learned early on that if our baby was going to sleep, and we gently patted them in a repetitive, soft manner on their tush, they went to sleep without any problem. I know it sounds strange, but it is a little secret put-baby-to-bed trick that works like a charm. There is something about that reassuring pat that babies love. To me, this is a reminder that the human need for touch is wired into us from birth. Touch is something we need and want, something essential for healthy living. Let's all remember to reach out and give a reassuring touch whenever we can.

Did you know that you don't even need a partner to engage in physical touch? You can touch yourself. (No, not in that way, but hey, if it works, maybe in that way too.) I'm simply referring to massaging yourself on different parts of your body.

I remember taking a yoga class years ago, and we were in a forward bend. The teacher said that we should reach over to our calves and massage them. I remember thinking, weird. But I did it. And it felt really good. Then, she said "As you stand up, continue massaging your knees, your thighs, hips and butt" (I swear she said that.)Then she had us do our arms and our neck and even our face. It was such an eye-opening experience because it felt so good, and I thought to myself, "Wow, I could have been doing this my whole life?" Sometimes you don't know until you know!

So for this section, we are not just talking about connection and touch with another person, we are also talking about doing it for yourself, too. After all, it's just as important (maybe even more) to love and nourish yourself as it is to love and nourish others.

BENEFITS OF CONNECTION

Touch Improves:
- sleep
- cardiovascular health
- muscle flexibility
- immune system
- oxytocin levels
- self-esteem
- feelings of trust
- feelings of safety

Touch Reduces:
- headaches and migraines
- tension
- muscle aches
- pain
- stress
- sadness
- sense of isolation
- feelings of loneliness
- angry thoughts

GORDON'S STORY

When I asked my friend Gordon to write a story for my book, he immediately said yes. I gave him a list of topics and within an hour he had sent me this deeply touching story. It makes me cry every time I read it. It reminds me that we are only here for a brief moment, and we must remind ourselves that these moments of touch and connection are all that really matter. Thank you, Gordon, for one of the most stunningly beautiful stories I have ever read. I love you, my friend.

A GLIMPSE OF ETERNITY BY GORDON MCARDLE

It was the best of times; it was the worst of times …My Dad died from cancer some years ago, and we had six weeks together in the hospital from when we were told he was going to die to his passing. I feel what a blessing this time was. Many people lose loved ones suddenly. We got to spend time together caring for him to the end. He was in good form with only a little pain and so it was a time that we could really be with each other.

One day after staying overnight in the hospital, I went home for some sleep. My mum and sister took over with my father. The time was coming, and we didn't want dad being alone. I wasn't home long when my sister called to say he was asking for me and to come as quickly as possible. I got to the hospital and ran to his room. I sat on the edge of his bed, and my mum and sister left the room. He said to me: "You remember when your grandad was sick?" And I did.

My mum's dad had died some years before having had a stroke. After the stroke he lived for two years, the family taking care of him at home. My dad's 'job' was to shave him. I saw him do it, and I remembered. He would sit in front of him on a stool and make jokes with him. My dad was good humored and had a gentle manner. I remember the respectful way he would treat his father-in-law, this once proud, upright man now debilitated by illness. I remembered thinking Granddad's dignity was in good hands. I loved my dad for that.

"I'd like you to shave me." My voice caught. The poignancy of this was not lost on me. This would be his last shave, part of the preparation for what was coming. I nodded and smiled, "Of course."

I went to the little bathroom and got his shaving gear. I got one of those little bowls and half-filled it with water, not too hot, just nice and warm, and I went back to the edge of his bed. I lathered up his face, gentle, like he was. And I shaved my dad. I remember taking such care, concentrating fully on what I was doing, each stroke easy and cautious, trying to get it just right. As I switched sides to shave the other side of his face, I caught his eye. He was gazing at me, and we smiled at each other. I had never felt more loved than at that moment. I finished and patted his face gently.

These few moments were some of the most intimate of my life.

THE EXERCISES

The first exercises are meant to be done with a partner while the final exercises are meant to be done without a partner.

CONNECTION WITH PARTNER

EXERCISE 1: PARTNER MASSAGE

Massage helps our body renew itself as it calms our nervous system. It is great for reducing stress and strengthening our immune system. Plus, it feels great!

THE TECIINIQUE

Decide if you will be giving or receiving the massage. Both feel great so make sure to try both roles. The person giving the massage should take a few relaxing breaths while the person receiving the massage gets comfortable. It's nice to have a blanket nearby to stay warm as you are receiving the massage. Massage oils are very nice to experiment with. Experiment with different scents to see which work best for you and your partner. If you plan to use massage oil, make sure it is placed next to your alarm clock so you are totally ready for this exercise.

You can hit the snooze button once, twice, or even more depending on how much time you have and what your morning routine looks like. If you are giving the massage, make sure you keep your back straight and refrain from bending too much. Try to use a very slow and regular pace and try not to use your thumbs too much. Remember to continue to breathe throughout the massage.

Here is a great five-minute massage routine with some tips to help you begin.

- Start at the shoulders. Gently massage the muscle part of the shoulders, on either side of the neck. Make sure to use your palms and try not to pinch with your fingers. Aim to squeeze the muscles between the fingers and the heel of the hand. It should feel similar to what you would do if you squeezed a lemon. Practice your technique, asking your partner how the sensations feel along the way. Continue to gently knead the muscles of the shoulders moving outwards until you get to the bony part of their shoulder. Stop here and move back to the neck and massage outwards one more time.

- Alternatively, you can take your thumbs and press down firmly on the muscle from either side of the neck down to the bony section of the shoulders. Firmly press the thumbs on either side for a few seconds before moving down one thumb width to the next section. You should be able to do about four to six compressions before you get to the bony section of the shoulder. Stop when you get to the bony section and repeat from the beginning.

- Move onto the neck area by making a C shape with your hand and placing it on the back of the neck. Use the lemon squeezing motion with your fingers and the heel of your palm to gently massage the neck.

- Moving onto the base of the skull, make sure you move any hair or jewelry out of the way. Stand to one side of them and then gently place one hand on their forehead and cup your other hand at the base of their skull. Using your fingers, make a small circular motion to knead the base of the skull gently. Continue doing this until you have covered the entire area. Repeat on the other side.

- For the final touches, gently begin to stroke down the back. Use sweeping motions on either side of the spine, avoiding the bony areas. You are aiming to sweep along the muscles to either side of the spine. If you still have more time, you can massage the muscles on either side of the spine using your thumbs or the heel of your hand. Experiment to see what feels good for your partner. If you are the one receiving the massage, make sure to communicate what feels great and what doesn't. This serves an added benefit of improving communication between you and your partner and allows each person to get comfortable expressing their wishes.

- This entire process should take about five minutes. It's such a great way to start the day, and you will both feel amazing afterwards. If you have time, hit that snooze a second time and switch places. How amazing would it be to start the day this way? You will feel good, and your partner will feel good. Also, not only will you be creating a great feeling of connection between you and your partner to start the day, but it sets the tone for the evening when you come back together. Who knows where that may lead? But I digress.

- Make sure to thank your partner and feel that gratitude towards them if you were the one receiving the massage. Take a few moments throughout the day to reflect upon how starting the day with a massage made you feel.

They slipped briskly into an intimacy
from which they never recovered.
—F. Scott Fitzgerald

EXERCISE 2: HUG AND TOUCH

Hugs increase happiness and make us healthier while reducing stress, anxiety, and pain. Unfortunately, many people in modern society are touch deprived. Busy lives, hectic schedules, and lots of responsibility leads to less opportunity to hug or even to exchange simple touches, like a touch on the arm or a quick pat on the back. Here is your chance to change all this, even before you get out of bed.

When your alarm rings, hit the snooze button and hug and cuddle with your significant other. If you are currently living alone, take this time to hug yourself. We're serious. Wrap your arms around a loved one or yourself. You can sweep your hands up and down your partner's arms or back, allowing your partner to do the same. This is a nice time to exchange sweet conversation and appreciation for one another, or you can lie in silence, enjoying the touch of your partner. Alternatively, play some soft, relaxing music, and enjoy your touch session this way.

Music enhances every experience. Go the extra mile and create a special playlist for these touch sessions filled with music that relaxes you and makes you feel good. Even better, create this playlist together with your partner. While you're at it, you can create a sexy playlist for those intimate moments between you and your partner. But that's a topic for another book. For now, create the playlists, touch, one another, and feel great.

Don't forget to use music, candles, and scent to enhance the experience. You can lie in bed, sit up or stand for these sessions. Experiment with all the different ways you can exchange loving touch.

Perhaps you would like to create your own touch ritual. It's nice to call it a ritual, to make it special and to tailor it to your own preferences. Working together to do this is a beautiful way to connect and communicate more with your partner.

> *Love is like breathing. You take it in and let it out.*
> —Wally Lamb

CONNECTION WITH SELF

EXERCISE 3: SELF MASSAGE

Have you ever spent a few minutes massaging your feet, legs, arms, or neck? If not, this will be a game changer for you. When your alarm sounds, sit up and do one of the following self-massage techniques. If you want to feel really good, take two or three snoozes to do a few of the techniques.

FOOT MASSAGE

Let's start with your feet. Your feet do a lot of work for you each day, carrying you around and taking the brunt of the surfaces you walk upon. We are meant to walk without shoes, so our feet can adjust to the terrain and move accordingly. Our feet have a lot of nerve endings which are there to monitor the ground we are walking on.

Unfortunately, most people spend the majority of their time in shoes. Shoes take away your ability to feel the ground. They also force your feet into an unnatural position as you walk. Most shoes have a hard sole which makes it unyielding. So the foot takes a beating. Let's start to take care of our feet with this massage technique.

Go to kerryfishercoaching.com for the video resource for this exercise.

The Technique

- Bend your knee and bring your foot as close to your body as you can. If you can bring it into your lap, do so, otherwise, place your foot in a position that allows you to reach the sole of your foot. Place one thumb under your big toe and the other under pinky toe and press firmly down into the flesh. Move your thumbs down directly below this spot on either side and then press firmly once again. Continue moving down in a line from your big toe down to your heel and from your pinky toe down to your heel, keeping your thumbs evenly lined up across your foot, one on each side. Once you reach your heel, you can do this once more or move on to the next section.
- Now, place one thumb below your second toe and one below your fourth toe. Press the spot directly below each toe with each thumb. Again, keep your thumbs lined up across the foot, one below each toe. Work down the foot to the heel and then repeat or move onto the next section.
- Take both thumbs and press them firmly below your middle toe, pressing firmly into the flesh. Continue working down towards

the heel, stopping to press firmly in each spot. When you get down to your heel, repeat or move on to the next section.

- Hold your foot with one hand and make a fist with the other. Lightly punch the soft part of the sole of the foot, the space between the ball of your foot and your heel. Experiment with the amount of pressure you use; your foot can take a lot of pressure. Try and see what feels right for you. It should feel good, and it should not hurt.

- Continuing to hold your foot in your hand, lace the fingers of one hand through the toes. This might be uncomfortable if you have never done this before. If it is uncomfortable, it means your toes have been squished into your shoes. Toes are meant to be splayed a bit to aid in walking but wearing shoes forces them to move inward. If this is the case for you, make it a daily practice to lace your fingers in between your toes and to walk without shoes as much as possible. Free your feet!

- As you massage your feet, take a moment to look at them closely. Your feet are perfectly designed to carry you around all day long. Here's a cool fact: each of your feet has 26 bones. That means that your feet account for about one fourth of the bones in your body. Pretty incredible, aren't they?

Arm and Leg Massage

- When the alarm clock sounds, grab some lotion and begin to massage your arms. Begin at your neck and massage the muscle there. Moving down to your shoulder, massage the big muscle there. Continue moving down your arm massaging your upper arm (front and back), your forearm (front and back), then move to your hand.

- Take some time here to massage your hand. Your hand, like your foot, does a ton of work for you each day, yet we never really pay much attention to it. Massage your palm and then each finger in turn. As you do so, admire the miracle that is your hand. Did you know that each of your hands has 27 bones? That means 54 bones out of the 206 in your body are in your hands.

- Here's an even more amazing statistic: almost half of the bones in your body are in your hands and your feet. Certainly, these masterpieces of architectural splendor are worth a little extra time, effort, and love. Wouldn't you agree?
- Time to move to your legs. Begin with your thigh and massage one thigh and then the other. Use a firm motion using your fingers and heel of your hand as if you were squeezing a lemon. Continue to work down your leg, massaging around your knees, to your shin and calf and then down to your foot, massaging your heels and then each toe. Wiggle your toes around a bit and shake out your legs.

Mirror Work

Have you ever heard of mirror work? If not, you are about to learn one of the greatest tools for creating an extraordinary life that exists. There are two different ways to do this mirror work, and we encourage you to try both; then, do the one that works best for you. Let's get to it.

Intimacy is a totally different dimension.
It is allowing the other to come into you,
to see you as you see yourself.
—Osho

EXERCISE 4: MIRROR WORK—SEVEN THINGS

- This is based on an exercise by motivational speaker Lisa Nichols. Get ready because this exercise is powerful, and it can bring up lots and lots of emotions. We suggest you do this for a minimum of 21 days although you can do it for longer. The longer you do it, the better you will feel.

- Sit in front of a mirror. Get comfortable. You will be speaking out loud so make sure you have some privacy when you do this exercise.
- Begin by telling yourself seven things that you love about yourself. Let the words flow and say whatever comes to mind.
- Next, tell yourself seven things you forgive yourself for.
- Finally, tell yourself seven things that you commit to yourself that you will do.
- Do this every day. It is perfectly fine to repeat the same things each day. The idea is to do it each and every day and to look yourself in the eyes as you say it.
- You might want to journal afterwards, especially if you feel emotional during the exercise.
- Write down what comes up for you, what emotions you feel, what thoughts you have during the exercise.
- Allow this exercise to work its magic on you. If you skip a day, don't worry, just continue on the following day. No need to start over!

Until you make peace with who you are,
you'll never be content with what you have.
—Doris Mortman

EXERCISE 5: MIRROR WORK—EYE GAZING

- Simply sit and look into your own eyes. The eyes are the window to the soul. Look into that window and see your soul. Appreciate who you are. Send love to yourself.
- Maybe even say it out loud... "I love you." Yes, it might feel weird but who cares? Weird? Maybe. Powerful? Definitely.

- As an extra step, you can take a few minutes to journal right after you gaze into your own eyes. Write down the emotions that come up, thoughts you have, how it feels to gaze into your eyes during the exercise.
- Challenge yourself to continue this practice.
- You could even do this as you brush your teeth each day. That's habit stacking at its best. More on that in a later chapter. For now, gaze and enjoy.

He who knows others is wise;
he who knows himself is enlightened.
—Lao Tzu

EXERCISE 6: VISUALIZATION—TO BE IN THE BODY

- Many of us live up in our heads and many more of us are completely disconnected from our bodies. Doing this simple exercise will help you to feel more centered and grounded.
- This may seem a bit weird, but trust us and just try it. It has been a game changer for us, and it might be for you too. When you hear the snooze button sound, turn it off, sit up and close your eyes. I know, I know, you just opened them but just try it.
- Ok, eyes are closed.
- Now, visualize yourself above your body.
- You can imagine it like a hologram or a shadow or a full picture of yourself floating above your physical body.
- Now, imagine that the body above you actually falls down into your physical body.
- As if you are falling down into your own self.
- See how that feels.
- Allow yourself to feel what it is like to be fully in your body.

How to Bring Connection into Your Day

While you are at work, gently massage your upper arms or your neck. You could get up and walk around your office or home when you start to feel tired, or you need an energy boost.

Anytime you are beginning to feel overwhelmed, stressed, unhappy in any way or when your thoughts are starting to run away from you, do the visualization exercise. This will get you out of your head and into your body where you belong.

When you see your family members or dear friends, give them a long, warm hug. Do some self-massage or partner massage before bed or before you lay down to sleep. Take a few moments throughout the day to massage your neck or your arms or your hands or all of the above. This is especially important if you are sitting for long periods in front of a computer.

Reflect

1. Think about ways you can bring more physical touch into your life. Can you hug people more, reach out and briefly rest your hand on their arm? Try it.
2. Observe what happens when you incorporate more touch into your day. See how you feel after you touch or exchange a hug with different people in your life.
3. Make a list of the times you typically get stressed and aim to replace that stress with a bit of physical touch.
4. What does it feel like to be in your body and what does it feel like when you are caught in your mind? Which feels better?
5. How do you feel when you increase the amount of connection time you have with your partner?
6. Which exercise feels best?

7. How would it feel if you incorporated this practice of exchanging loving touch with your partner, friends, family members?

> *I've learned that every day you should reach*
> *out and touch someone. People love a warm hug,*
> *or just a friendly pat on the back.*
> —Maya Angelou

Look deep into nature, and then you will understand everything better.

—ALBERT EINSTEIN

CHAPTER 11

GET OUT IN NATURE

Keep close to nature's heart...and break clear away,
once in a while, and climb a mountain or spend a
week in the woods. Wash your spirit clean.
—John Muir

*M*y younger sisters and I always loved hunting butterflies when we were young. We didn't have a butterfly net, so we used to take our mother's strainer, the one she used to drain spaghetti, and we would head out into the fields. We would wait patiently until a butterfly alighted on a flower, and then we would slowly move in, capture it, and place it gently in a jar. After we had a few butterflies in our jar, we would set them free and start all over.

One day, we came home with a gorgeous blue butterfly in our jar. We showed it to our mom and she was delighted. She told us that when she was a child, she too, would run after and capture butterflies. We were entranced by this story of a younger version of our mom chasing butterflies. You don't often think about your mom as a child.

My mom paused and then told us that she actually collected bugs when she was a child. She would mount them on cardboard and frame them. I was puzzled as I pondered this idea. How could you mount a bug? I asked her and to my horror, she said that all you had to do was to stick a pin in the butterflies head so you could preserve it perfectly with the wings spread open. Apparently she and my grandfather, a landscaper, would do this as a hobby.

I was horrified by what I had just heard. My mom asked me if I wanted to collect butterflies and I very quickly told her no. There was no way I was sticking any needles in a butterfly's head and I wasn't about to let her do it either. I grabbed the jar and ran out the back door, all the way back into the woods and I set the butterfly free. I never again brought a butterfly home. We knew now that the butterfly killer lived in our house lol!

When I became a mom, I wanted to bring my love of butterflies to my kids and perhaps, looking back, to make up for my mother's childhood pursuits, I created a yearly ritual. We would purchase caterpillars, feed them, watch them grow, watch them cocoon, and then emerge as beautiful butterflies. My kids loved watching this incredible process, and so did I. The best part was always when the kids would set them free. They would wait patiently for the butterfly to walk onto their finger and then they would set it free. Watching the butterflies fly off into the sky reminds me of my childhood and those butterfly hunting days with my sisters.

Spending time in nature is one of the most impactful ways to start your day. Our modern society is very sedentary. Most of us spend a majority of our time indoors. With the advent of television and computers, there's always so much to do inside, and we often forget all the amazing things we could be doing outside. Let's change our ideas about how to live our lives by spending a few minutes outdoors as soon as the alarm rings.

Many of us spend the majority of our lives indoors breathing air that is stale, recycled, and quite frankly, unhealthy for us. Poor indoor air quality can lead to infections, lung cancer, and even chronic lung diseases like asthma. We are meant to be outdoors, with the sun upon us, breathing fresh air. Spending time outdoors strengthens your immunity, calms your mind, and increases your longevity.

When you spend a substantial amount of time indoors, your body misses out on the opportunity to engage with a variety of environments. This actually makes your immune system weaker. A 2010 study focused on the benefits of spending time out in nature. During the study, a group of adults took a three-day trip to the forest. The study showed that as a result of the trip, the number of white blood-cells in their blood increased and remained elevated for more than 30 days. White blood cells play an important role in immune health. Our bodies are meant to be subjected to different environments with varying fluctuations in temperature. It makes us stronger and conditions our bodies to function at peak levels. So, let yourself go out in the hot weather, the cold weather, the rain, and even the snow. Doing this will make your body more resilient and reduce stress by lowering blood pressure and reducing stress levels in your body.

Spending time in nature has been shown to relieve stress in teens and adults. A Chinese study followed a group of male students who spent their break from school camping and hiking. What they found was these students returned with lower levels of the stress hormone cortisol. This is yet another example of how spending time in nature makes you healthy, both physically and mentally. And let's face it; is there anything more relaxing than having the wind in your face and being surrounded by nature in all her majesty?

In nature my heart
beats with the rhythm beyond
soothing my body.
—Dani Glasser

BENEFITS OF NATURE

Nature Increases:
- brain function
- mental clarity
- creativity
- levels of vitamin D (immune system regulator)
- peace of mind

Nature Reduces:
- blood pressure
- anxiety
- depression
- mental health issues
- cortisol levels (stress hormone)

A NATURAL SHIFT BY DANI GLASSER

Whenever I am in nature, I notice a shift in my body. I slow down, notice how my senses connect with the environment. Feeling the wind on my skin—pleasant on a hot day, and a bit jarring when it is cold. Smelling the scent of rain, damp earth, or the crispness before it snows.

As I walk, my vision is delighted by the trees, grass, clouds in the sky. Even in my home, I open the curtains so I can see the green (or snow) depending on the day as I find it incredibly soothing.

When my beloved became ill, and I was living between two states with the kiddos, nature became a grounding point. When I was apart from him, I would start my mornings curled up on the couch with tea, in a fuzzy robe and just look out the window at the backyard to calm my brain before anything else. In the afternoons, I would get out and walk so that I could move my body freely and expansively, open myself up and after being closed ini all day. While walking, I spent a lot of time looking at the sky, literally infusing my body with the expansiveness. If it was nice out, and we were together, then we would sit in the sun and talk.

Since then, being in nature, on some level every day has become a priority. I make it a point to get outside for as long as I can, breathe it in, and then surround myself with photos of it. During some of my darkest hours, nature has soothed my heart and soul, simply by it's presence or even a photo. If I am stressed, simply thinking about my favorite spot, looking at a photo, or a walk calms my nervous system immediately.

THE EXERCISES

EXERCISE 1: ENJOY NATURE

We want to get more fresh air into our lives, more time spent admiring the beauty of nature all around us, and more time getting in touch with our mother Earth. Use all your senses for this exercise.

PRACTICE

- The simplest way to do this technique is to wake up, hit the snooze button, and then go to your window. Open it and breathe deeply while gazing outside at the beauty unfolding in front of you.
- If it is early morning, go to a window where you can see the sunrise or to a window where the moon may still be peeking down at you.
- You can check out different windows in your home, observing the beauty that is in each one. You might be surprised to notice that there are some windows you have never ever looked out before. Here's your chance. This provides such a beautiful opportunity to see things in a different light. Enjoy the view!
- As you gaze out the window, think about these questions:
- What do you see?

- What do you hear?
- What do you smell?
- What does the air feel like on your face?
- How do you feel in your body when you look outside?
- What are the quality of your thoughts as you gaze outdoors?

We do not see nature with our eyes,
but with our understandings and our hearts.
—William Hazlitt

EXERCISE 2: OBSERVE NATURE

For this technique, turn off your alarm and head directly outside.

PRACTICE

- Sit or stand, walk or lie. The idea is to allow your body to be in a natural setting, connected to nature.
- Observe what you observe and be in nature.
- Think about how you feel as you immerse yourself in the beauty around you.
- As you breathe in the fresh air, think to yourself, "Relax, relax, relax."
- Notice the quality of your thoughts as you embrace the world around you.
- Feel how you are connected to everything around you.

Note: If you have started to do more than one Snooze Button Session each morning, do the techniques like meditation and journaling first and then head outside.

Adopt the pace of nature: her secret is patience.
—Ralph Waldo Emerson

EXERCISE 3: SENSES IN NATURE

This is a beautiful exercise to tap into your senses. When you pause to really take in what you see, what you hear, what you smell, what you feel, it helps you connect with your body on a whole new level. In day to day life, you can easily forget to tune into your senses. This exercise will help you to reconnect with your senses, drop into your body and rediscover the magic of the world around you.

- Turn off the alarm and head outside.
- Sit down in a comfortable place.
- Breathe calmly and quietly and look around.
- What do you see?
- Observe everything that you see, saying to yourself... "I see the sky," "I see the trees." Continue to observe and say what you see.
- Close your eyes and listen. What do you hear? As you hear each sound, tell yourself what you are hearing, "I hear a bird chirping." "I hear the wind blowing."
- Turn your attention to your sense of smell. What can you smell? As you smell each scent, describe it to yourself. "I smell flowers that remind me of roses." "I smell the sweet grass that reminds me of childhood."
- Stand up and walk over to a tree or grass. Feel the tree or grass and describe how it feels. "This grass feels soft." "The tree feels rough."
- As you finish the exercise, turn in a circle and look at everything you can see. Look around you, below you, above you. Throw your arms out and feel grateful for this moment, grateful for the beauty of nature, grateful to be alive.

In every walk with nature, one receives far more than he seeks.
—John Muir

EXERCISE 4: EXTENDED MORNING ROUTINE

This is for the days when you have a few extra minutes, the days when you have time to get up 15 minutes to an hour early. When the alarm goes off, instead of hitting the snooze button, you turn off the alarm, grab a drink and head outside.

PRACTICE

- Grab a smoothie, juice, cup of coffee or tea, and make the experience beautiful.
- This could become a lovely morning ritual that you do alone or with a special person like your mate, your children. or even one of your pets.
- Either find a comfortable space within your home or head outside to enhance the experience.
- Sit down and take a deep breath.
- Take the time to savor your drink, the space you are in if you are inside or the beautiful nature around you if you are outside.
- As an addition to this peaceful practice, you can bring your journal and spend a few minutes journaling and drinking, savoring these calm moments before the chaos of the day begins.
- Bring this sense of peace and calm into your day.

Time spent amongst trees is never time wasted.
—Katrina Mayer

EXERCISE 5: GET ACTIVE OUTDOORS

This is another practice for those days when you have more time. Turn off your alarm clock and get outside. The idea is to get moving so you can take a walk or put on some music and dance or do any movement that works for you. Incorporating more time outdoors is a great way to add a sense of connection to your life. This is especially important if you spend most of your day indoors working. Just a few moments of fresh air could change your mood, your health and your attitude.

PRACTICE

- Head outside and
  - o exercise
  - o do yoga
  - o meditate
  - o practice some breathing techniques
  - o do a walking meditation by slowly placing one foot in front of the other, noticing every movement, every step

> *My wish is to stay always like this,*
> *living quietly in a corner of nature.*
> —Claude Monet

HOW TO BRING NATURE INTO YOUR DAY

There are many opportunities throughout the day to spend a few minutes outdoors. You could head outdoors during your lunch break and eat your lunch, picnic style, on the grass outside. Keep a blanket in your car for these impromptu outdoor meals. Increase the benefit by asking a co-worker to join you. It's a beautiful way to bond outside of the typical work environment.

After you finish work, take a quick walk before jumping into your car. Or you could drive straight to a park or lake or other area of natural beauty and spend a short time there, breathing deeply, and enjoying your surroundings. Perhaps you could even take the time here for a brisk walk or hike. You could also drive home, change, and ask your significant other or one of your kids to take a quick walk with you. After dinner, you could create a ritual where you have a solitary walk or a family walk.

There are so many ways you could add time outdoors into your life, get creative! Do what makes you feel good. Begin to think about some outdoor activities you enjoy. You could add hiking, biking, swimming, paddle boarding, golfing, or outdoor tennis into your life. The outdoor activity possibilities are endless. Get creative and get outside!

REFLECT

1. Reflect on the ways spending more time outdoors would benefit you. Then commit to an outdoor lifestyle.
2. Make a list of times throughout the day and week that you could fit in some outdoor time. Pick one and begin.
3. What outdoor activities did you love as a child? Journal about this to rediscover some of the things you enjoyed as a child. Who knows, you may still enjoy these things.
4. What outdoor activity would you enjoy as an adult today? Commit to discovering at least one outdoor activity that you could add into your life.
5. Who would you like to do this outdoor activity with? Make a list of people whom you think might enjoy joining you and then reach out to one of them and set up your first activity together.

CHURNING, TUMBLING, ROLLING IN THE WAVES

I have always loved the outdoors. The sun on my face, the wind in my hair, the birds and butterflies fluttering around, the trees and flowers swaying gently in the breeze. To me, it's pure heaven.

Every summer my sisters and I went to my grandmother's house in Fort Lauderdale, Florida for the month of August. We spent our days languishing by the community pool, sitting amidst the palm trees, playing shuffle board and backgammon, and splashing around in the pool. I truly loved those lazy days in the sun.

For a week every summer, our grandparents would take us to Sanibel Island, so we could spend time at the beach. My sisters and I would wake up, run to the beach and then swim out right past the spot where the waves were breaking, so we could gently float up and down as the waves came in. We spent hours out there. I remember the feeling to this day. The sun, shimmering in a golden line across the water, glinting like a golden path to infinity. The water coming in, wave after wave, one after the other. As the wave came in, we would gently bob up and over, buoyed by the water.

Every once in a while, though, a rogue wave would come and instead of simply lifting us up and allowing us to bob over it, the wave would crash early, up and over our heads. We learned to hold our breath and dive deep down when that happened to avoid being pummeled by the wave. Every once in a while, though, we misjudged and the wave got us, and we would be grabbed by the wave, churned along with it. I remember those waves because it was scary when that happened. Everything was a blur, under the water, unable to breathe and I couldn't tell which way was up, We learned that if we didn't panic but, instead, relaxed and allowed the wave to take us, we would be tumbled around quite a bit but eventually we would be deposited, safe and sound, by the shore.

I think about those rogue waves often. I learned so much from those waves, I learned that sometimes you have no control over things, and you have to simply hold your breath, relax, and allow. I learned that it's important to never panic when you are in a difficult situation. I learned that things usually end up ok in the end. Those lazy days in Florida cemented my love of the beach, of the sun and sea, of nature itself in all its majesty.

Fast forward 30 years and I found myself taking my kids to Florida for the summer every year. We would relocate to the beach and spend the days collecting shells, building sand castles, and walking along the shore. Each day, I would watch my kids as they waded out into the sea and bobbed there, just beyond the breakpoint, chatting, laughing, bonding. And every once in a while, one of them would get grabbed by a wave and tumble to the shore where I would be waiting for them to pick them up, give them a little reassurance and then send them back out there. History has a beautiful way of repeating itself sometimes, doesn't it? The memories of my childhood would blend with the new memories I was making with my children there on the beach, and in those moments, all was right with my world. Nature never disappoints.

Live in the sunshine, swim in the sea, drink the wild air.
—Ralph Waldo Emerson

One day at a time...and life becomes sublime.

—Louise Hay

CHAPTER 12

AFFIRMATIONS, VISUALIZATIONS, AND SELF-LOVE

I am visualizing a perfect world
where everyone is living in harmony
and experiencing their life purpose to the fullest.
—Jack Canfield

ARI'S STORY

Two years after my second child was born, we found out we were pregnant with our third child. At 26 weeks into my pregnancy, I lost the baby. I had to deliver our baby, knowing he would never take his first breath. It was the worst experience of my entire life. When you deliver a stillborn baby, you still deliver the baby on the same floor that everyone else is delivering. So I spent hours listening to the sounds of babies coming into the world, listening to their first cries. I knew my baby would never make a sound. It was devastating. I went numb. I remember the disconnection I felt from the entire situation; I was in shock, in grief.

When the baby was born, we held him for a few hours. It was shocking to see such a perfect baby, so tiny yet still. We named him Ari. We kissed him, we held him, we said goodbye to him. It was a terrible time for me, but I knew I had to keep functioning for my two little boys. Every morning when I woke up, I felt crushing sadness. I felt paralyzed.

I would sit up in bed and begin, "Kerry, you are strong. It's ok to be sad now, but you will get through this. You are strong. You will feel better soon. You are strong. You can do this." I would repeat those words until I could get up and function. It worked.

As I went through my day, whenever I started to feel that constriction in my chest or the feeling that I couldn't go on, I would begin again. Silently repeating to myself, "You are strong. You can do this. You are strong. You will feel better soon. You are strong." I did this for almost a year, until the day that my son Tanner was born, and I could breathe freely once more. Those affirmations saved me.

We already discussed creative visualization in an earlier chapter. Another way to use visualization is to begin an affirmation and lofty question practice. If you have never heard of affirmations or lofty questions, get ready to add powerful value to your life. If you have heard of them but think that they are silly, new age nonsense, then get ready to open your mind.

Speaking of the mind, let's take a closer look at the brain. Your brain is the most powerful computer that exists. Your brain is a magnificent masterpiece, a technological wonder. Your brain has one job—to keep you alive. In order to do this, your brain is constantly scanning your surroundings looking for danger. When it spots danger, the brain's job is to move you away from that danger. The brain wants to move you away from pain and towards pleasure. Sounds great, doesn't it? Well, not so fast.

Let's see how this works. The brain is constantly surveying your surroundings to see if there is anything that could pose a danger to you. The brain does this by gathering information with your senses. Your sense of sight, hearing, smell, touch, and taste are all there as a way to gather information from your surroundings and to relay that information to the brain. The brain then analyzes the information and takes action. That's all good, right? Well, maybe; maybe not.

It turns out that the brain is not very discerning when it comes to what it deems safe and what it deems unsafe. If you were late to work and stuck in traffic, your body would pump the same chemicals into your body as it would if you were confronted by a lion. The brain sees both of these as a danger and, in both cases, your sympathetic nervous system is activated. When the sympathetic nervous system is activated, your body releases adrenaline and noradrenaline into your system. As a result, your heart rate and blood pressure increase to prepare you for the impending danger. This is what gives you the ability to fight or run. When you fight or run, your body uses those chemicals and they dissipate. However, when you are sitting in traffic and flooded with those chemicals, and without the ability to fight or run, the chemicals stay in your body, and this has a negative impact on your physiology.

This is an automatic response, and it creates a cascade of behaviors that allows you to get ready to fight, flee, or freeze. This is how your body protects you. This system works well when we are in danger, however, it doesn't work well when we are not in actual danger. Since your brain is always on guard, trying to protect you, you tend to notice and think about the negative things in your surroundings. Your brain quite literally has a negativity bias, as it searches for clues that indicate danger. You will always notice a lot more of the negative things than the positive things. It's simply how you are wired. Noticing all the negative can lead to that stress response which floods the body with stress hormones. This can create feelings of anxiety, excessive worry, and fear in situations that don't call for this.

The brain is a very efficient machine. When we think about things repeatedly, the neural circuits for those things get wired in. There is a saying, first coined by Donald Hebbs, "neurons that fire together wire together." This basically means that whatever we think about expands. The way your brain works is as you have a thought, the brain sends the message along neural pathways. The more you think that thought, the stronger the neural pathway becomes. The brain quite literally wires the neurons together for those thoughts that you have repeatedly. The other part of this is the brain cleans up the neural pathways that are not used. Think about what this means. The pathways that are used often get wired in while the ones that are not used are discarded.

Add in the idea that our brain is wired for negativity, and you will see why learning to replace the negative thoughts with positive thoughts will help you to rewire your brain. We want the positive thoughts to get wired in, not the negative thoughts. There is a lot of research being done to investigate this further and the research reinforces this idea. What was once in the realm of the spiritual seekers, this idea that we can create the thoughts we want to have, feel the emotions we want to feel, and to live in the state we want to be in has now come into the mainstream.

The best thing is that it's free and you have nothing to lose. So why not try it? It might just change what you think about, and changing what you think about changes who you are.

KANIKA'S STORY

I have always been an ardent believer of the Divine/God whatever one wants to call it. Family prayers were always done daily and it became a habit eventually. It was something I felt missing if I skipped it.

But the true meaning of prayer, devotion, and channeling came to me in 2018. I was devastated mentally, physically, and emotionally because of my abusive marriage. I was in the midst of a separation, and I was in a deep period of reflection.

The teacher then appeared in the form of Mindvalley believe it or not. I went on to learn from different authors, and I now affirm every morning, meditate in the middle of work, and pray each and every night. It gives me sooo much happiness really. It truly opened newer channels to me.

Here is the prayer I say each day:

I AM the Divine Power of Source
The Flame of Love
The Wings of Freedom
The Song of Joy
The Heart of the New Golden Age
Rise and Shine my Love!!

EXERCISES

EXERCISE 1: AFFIRMATIONS

An affirmation is a positive statement that you use to bring what you want into your life. We use positive affirmations to create that positive feedback loop in the brain, to help us rewire our thinking patterns. Affirmations are a great way to construct the vision of yourself that you imagine, to imagine the career you have always dreamed of, and to craft the life of your dreams. The definition of affirmation is "the action or process of affirming something or being affirmed, a positive assertion." So for this exercise, you will be creating the affirmations and then repeating them to yourself daily.

For this exercise, you should create a list of affirmations that you can use each day. Write them all down on a piece of paper that you keep next to your bed or write a note on your phone or on your computer. For even more impact, record your affirmations on your phone and listen to them during your Snooze Button Session. There is no sound sweeter than hearing your own voice telling you all about what you want to create in your life. Remember to create your list of affirmations the day before you need to use them for your Snooze Button Session. Keep it next to your bed, right next to your alarm clock, so you are ready to go when the alarm rings.

PRACTICE

- Press the Snooze Button and grab your affirmations.
- Either read them silently to yourself or for even greater impact, speak them out loud.
- Feel the emotions that arise when you speak out these affirmations.
- Remove any negative self-talk during this process. If a thought distracts you, gently bring your attention back to your list of affirmations and continue to go over them.
- Continue until the alarm sounds once more.

AFFIRMATIONS

- I am an abundant being.
- Every day in every way, I am getting better and better.
- My life is a beautiful masterpiece created by me and me alone.
- I can be, do, and have anything I imagine.
- I have perfect health.
- I love my body and appreciate its strength, vibrancy, and vitality.
- I honor myself every day, in every way.
- I am enough.
- New doors open up to me each and every day.
- I attract health, wealth, and abundance in all areas of my life.
- I can do anything I set my mind to.
- Everything is for my highest good.
- I forgive myself; I forgive others. I live from a place of understanding we are all human.
- I am the very best version of myself.
- I am a money magnet.
- I am respected and loved and rewarded for my efforts.
- I am grateful for... (fill in the blank).
- I am loving, kind, and thoughtful.

- I attract everything I want in life.

Am I good enough?
Yes, I am.
—Michelle Obama

EXERCISE 2: LOFTY QUESTIONS

Lofty Questions are similar to affirmations in that they are aimed at rewiring your brain. Lofty Questions are questions you pose to yourself such as, "Why does money flow to me with such ease?" Notice, this is similar to the affirmation, "Money flows to me with ease," however, instead of making a statement, you are posing it as a question. Why is this important? Well, it all goes back to how the brain works.

The brain's primary job is to keep you safe but its secondary job is to create the things in life that you want to create, to construct the world you want to construct. The brain does this by responding to your thoughts. Affirmations are great, however, if you don't believe the statement you are making, it is possible that your thinking patterns will make you respond, "Well, that's not true." At which point the affirmation is rejected. Lofty Questions are different because you aren't asserting a fact. Instead, you are asking for the thing you want. This is an incredible technique because the brain will immediately get to work to bring that into form.

Can we dip back into science for a moment? I promise to keep it short and simple. Let me introduce you to the Reticular Activating System, or RAS. The RAS is a weblike part of the brain that starts at the top of the spinal column, at the brain stem, and extends upwards into the brain. This is the part of the brain that acts like a filter, making sure that only the information we need is relayed to your brain. Remember, the senses gather information from our surroundings and then relay it to the brain. There is so much information out there that if you actually had to process all of it, the brain would get overloaded with too much input. The RAS acts like a filtering system that selects the pieces of information that are essential for you, only what you need to know to keep you safe and what you need to create the life you imagine.

Once the RAS filters the information, it then brings the information you need into the brain, activating the entire cerebral cortex and increasing the levels of arousal within the brain. This primes the brain and allows the brain to interpret the incoming information, so it can then take appropriate action. How incredible is this? The senses bring in the information, the RAS filters out what is unnecessary and then the necessary information is relayed to the brain, lighting up the cerebral cortex on the way. Then, the brain assesses the information and takes the action needed. Our brain is picking out just the things we need to keep safe and that are important to our lives while filtering out everything else. In a real way, we are constructing reality. Our senses pick up information and then in the dark vault of our mind, we construct a picture of the surroundings. Every single thing is happening within your brain.

So what information gets through the Reticular Activating System? The information that always gets through is the information that our brain considers important including threats to us or those we love, anything to do with sex, and we will also always notice when someone says our name. The other information that typically gets through is anything that we are interested in at that time, anything that our brain is currently working on or thinking about. This is why it is so important to pay attention to what we are thinking about. It is also the reason that Lofty Questions work. When you pose these questions to your brain, your brain begins to scan for information in our surroundings pertinent to these questions. Unlike affirmations that can be rejected by the brain as false, lofty questions simply pose the question and then the brain does what it needs to create that vision.

I first learned about Lofty Questions from Christie Marie Sheldon. She uses this technique to manifest everything she wants in life, and she teaches her clients and students to do the same. Christie says that a lofty question is a question that is posed in a positive manner which helps to direct your focus while at the same time, challenging your subconscious mind to search to make the statement come true. So, these questions can focus the Reticular Activating System to search your surroundings to find the pieces of information needed to make the statement come true.

Sounds pretty good, right? You might as well try it and see how it works. For this exercise, create the lofty questions the day before you begin this practice and write them down somewhere easy to find, preferably on a piece of paper next to your bed so when the alarm rings, you can simply pick it up and begin to read the lofty questions. You can use some of the lofty questions from the list below or create your own. Many people begin by simply using the ones below and then eventually create their own. Do what works for you.

PRACTICE

- Hit the Snooze Button and grab your list of Lofty Questions.
- Begin to read your Lofty Questions out loud.
- Notice how you feel when you say these questions out loud and try to connect with the feeling.
- You can also sit in front of a mirror and read the Lofty Questions out loud while looking at yourself in the mirror for a much more powerful experience.
- Continue reading your questions out loud until the alarm rings once again and then go on with your day.

LOFTY QUESTIONS

Health
- Why is my body a beautiful, fit, strong masterpiece?
- Why do I have the body of an athlete?
- Why do I always eat nourishing foods?

- Why do I work out each day with such ease and joy?
- Why am I able to be fully active and healthy all the days of my life?
- Why do I get stronger and healthier each day?

Wealth

- Why does money flow to me with such ease?
- Why am I able to stay in all the best hotels around the world when I travel?
- Why am I financially free to do whatever I want in life?
- Why do I always have financial abundance?
- Why do I get paid for doing what I love?
- Why does my money multiply so quickly?

Relationships

- Why is my love relationship so incredible?
- Why is my relationship with my family members so deep and intimate?
- Why am I surrounded by such amazing friends?
- Why am I always supported by my family and friends?
- Why am I such a good... (friend, lover, coworker, parent, boss)?
- Why am I surrounded by such uplifting people in all areas of my life?
- Why do I have such an amazing family?

Career

- Why does my career fill me with such joy and pleasure?
- Why am I able to work from anywhere in the world?
- Why does my job give me so much happiness and fulfillment?
- Why am I able to work and make money in a job that seems like play?
- Why do I love my coworkers so much?
- Why are my coworkers and I able to get so much work done with so much ease?

Quality of Life
- Why am I able to travel the world and have such amazing adventures?
- Why do I always have so many amazing experiences?
- Why is my home so beautiful and filled with such beautiful things?
- Why do I own beautiful homes around the world?
- Why do I always have so much fun?

Life Vision
- Why am I able to give so powerfully to the world?
- Why am I able to live a life of passion, mission, and fun?
- Why can I live where I want, when I want, and do anything I want?
- Why do I always live in flow?
- Why am I living my dream life?
- Why do I feel so grateful for all the blessings in my life?

If I had an hour to solve a problem and my life depended on
the solution, I would spend the first 55 minutes determining the
proper questions to ask, for once I know the proper question,
I could solve the problem in less than 5 minutes.
—Albert Einstein

FINAL NOTES

As with all the practices in this book, make sure to go easy on yourself, especially if this is the first time you are practicing the new techniques. It is ok if you feel resistance to this exercise or if you feel silly for sitting there repeating affirmations and lofty questions. Be gentle with yourself as you learn to rewire your brain. Remember, by rewiring for positive thoughts instead of negative thoughts, we are going against our biology, we are changing. As you allow your outdated ways of thinking to be replaced by new, more productive ways of thinking, be kind to yourself. Remember that change is always hard at first but, in the end, it is magnificent.

All change is hard at first, messy in the middle
and so gorgeous at the end.
—Robin Sharma

How to Bring Affirmations and Lofty Questions into Your Day

Now it's time to bring these practices into your day. Decide if you prefer affirmations or lofty questions. Ask yourself which one feels more authentic to you. Once you decide, make a list of your affirmations or lofty questions and place it on the mirror where you brush your teeth each day. Every time you stand by this mirror, read through the list. You can also add this list to your phone notes and read them once a day, maybe twice a day, maybe throughout the day. You might also record them and then listen back to this recording a few times a day. A great time to listen to your recording is when you are commuting to work and back. Prime your brain for action.

Reflect

1. How do you normally think about things? Are your thoughts generally positive or negative?
2. If your thoughts are usually negative, can you think about anyone in your life who thought this way as well? We often get our thinking patterns from parents, teachers, friends, and society. Where did you get yours?
3. How would you like to feel each day? Journal about this and then decide how you need to think if you want to feel that way. This

can motivate you to focus on your lofty questions and affirmations and take this practice seriously.

4. What are some of your hopes and dreams? Incorporate these into your affirmations and lofty questions.

5. Remember the brain dump? Do one now, listing all the things you ever wanted to accomplish, all the things you wanted to do in your life. Make sure to list the adventures you want to have, the career you dream of, the relationships you want to have, the home you want to live in, the toys you want to buy. Let your imagination soar here as you let yourself dream your biggest dreams about yourself and your life. Once that is done, look at the list and create tailored affirmations and lofty questions that help you move powerfully in the direction of your dreams.

I am the greatest.
I said that even before
I knew I was.

—Muhammed Ali

CHAPTER 13

IDEAL SELF

My mission in life is not merely to survive, but to thrive;
and to do so with some passion, some compassion,
some humor, and some style.
—Maya Angelou

CRAFTING MY DREAM LIFE

A few years ago, I went through a life-changing course called Lifebook. In all honesty, it was less of a course and more of an experience. Lifebook challenged me to take a serious look at 12 key areas of my life. I was able to create my perfect vision for my health and fitness, spiritual life, intellectual life, career, parenting, and social life, just to name a few. It felt as if no stone was left unturned. I examined every single aspect of my life. In the end, I created a 200-page book detailing my ideal self, my ideal life, my ideal everything!

Within two years of writing my very own Lifebook and examining every aspect of my life, massive positive changes had occurred. It was truly magical. I was living my dream life. Now, it's time to rewrite my vision for the next chapter of my life. I'm going even bigger this time because I'm a true believer in the idea that first you dream it, then you can achieve it.

Have you ever imagined what the ideal version of yourself would be like? If not, let's start now. It's very important to have a clear idea of who you want to be in the future. Having a clear vision of your ideal future self becomes the destination that you are aiming at. Yet, we are never taught to imagine who we want to become and how we want to transform. Without envisioning your better future self, you will stay exactly where you are.

Now, some of you might be thinking, "Well, I'm a grown adult. I have a good life. I like myself. I'm fine the way I am." And if that's you, I congratulate you. But I also challenge you. I challenge you to create a new, grander version of the person you have become. If you aren't one of the people who loves where you are in life, I challenge you to visualize your ideal life, so you can begin moving towards this vision.

Think about it, wouldn't it be exciting to aim at a more amazing you? Think about all the things you would need to learn and how fun the journey would be to get there. If your answer is, "No thank you, I am busy enough as it is. I don't have time to learn anything new. I'm content with getting by as I am." Ok, I hear that; I get you. But again, I challenge you. What if your life could become more exciting and filled with all the dreams you could possibly imagine? Dreams? You may be thinking. Who has time for that? With my career, my relationships, my family, and all the adulting that I'm forced to do, who has time to dream? And this, my friends, is what I seek to change.

When you were a child, you were always daydreaming. You were thinking about what you would become, who you would be. And then what happened? You grew up; you began to have responsibilities. Then, more responsibilities. Then, you got tired and perhaps overwhelmed. Well, I am going to challenge you one more time!

What if you aren't overwhelmed at all? What if you are actually *underwhelmed*? Doing the same thing all day every day, just trying to get to the weekend is boring and tedious and not exactly inspiring.

It's time to start dreaming again. It is time to start dreaming and tapping into all the things you hope to be and all the adventures you want to live. You deserve the best possible version of yourself you can dream up, and I am going to not only help you dream that person up, I am going to help you actually become that person!

Do not follow where the path may lead.
Go instead where there is no path and leave a trail.
—Ralph Waldo Emerson

BENEFITS OF ENVISIONING YOUR IDEAL SELF

Envisioning Your Ideal Self Improves:
- motivation
- inspiration
- focus
- visualization skills
- thoughts about the future

Envisioning Your Ideal Self Reduces:
- overwhelm
- boredom
- stress

THE EXERCISES

EXERCISE 1: THREE YEARS FROM NOW (JOURNAL)

Ok, the snooze button sounds; time to do some dreaming. If you have the time to do the entire exercise, hit the snooze button a few more times and complete it. Otherwise, break it down and do the exercise over a period of a few days.

Grab your journal or your computer, and let's get to work. Answer these questions and do so without giving it much thought. Allow yourself to free-write whatever comes to mind and then read it back to yourself.

PRACTICE

- Imagine yourself three years from now. Your life is exactly the way you want it to be. You have the perfect job, the perfect relationships, and your dream home.
- Everything is as it would be if your every wish were granted.
- Don't let any doubts creep in here, let that go, and allow the dream to unfurl.
- In this dream life of yours...
  o Who would you need to be to live a life like that?
  o How would you speak?
  o How would you dress?
  o How would you behave?
  o How would you treat people?
  o How would people feel after they spent time with you?
  o What time would you wake up?
  o What would you do when you wake up?
  o What would your workday look like?
  o Who would you eat your meals with?
  o Who would you spend your time with?
  o Who would you be if you could be the next grandest version of yourself in three years?
- **Present Day You**
  o *One simple action:* Keeping in mind who you want to be in three years, what is one step you can take today to move

powerfully in the direction of that person you dream of being? Challenge yourself to take this step today.

- o *List:* Make a list of simple actions you can take to up-level your health, your mind, your skills, your attitude, and your life. Pick one of these and do it today.
- Another way to do this exercise is to simply record the answers into your phone and then listen back when you can. You might surprise yourself with the things that get on the list!

> *You are never too old to set another goal*
> *or to dream a new dream.*
> —C.S. Lewis

EXERCISE 2: INNER CHILD PAST, PRESENT, AND FUTURE

- Read these questions and then record the answers using a voice recorder. You can also do this exercise as a journaling exercise.
- Allow yourself to speak freely, letting the words flow without overthinking.
- What hobbies did you have as a child?
- What did you spend a lot of your time doing as a kid?
- Did you play an instrument, write, paint, dance, sing? These are clues.
- What are the things you do presently that spark true joy within you?
- When do you feel most alive?
- Have you ever had a moment that felt just perfect?
  - o Where were you?
  - o What were you doing?
- Think about your future self.
  - o What would you like to be doing in three years?
  - o Five years?
  - o Ten years?

- o Continue into the future as far as you can.
- In order to be doing that in three years, five years, ten years, what skills do you need to learn?
  - o What habits do you need to instill?
  - o What practices do you need to put into place?
- Who do you need to spend time with?

No matter where you're from, your dreams are valid.
—Lupita Nyong'o

EXERCISE 3: MEDITATION FUTURE VERSION OF YOU LOOKING BACK

You can go to: kerryfishercoaching.com to access a full Future Self Guided Visualization.

This exercise is an overview for you in case you want to create your own tailored visualization for yourself. Simply record yourself on your phone as you go through this exercise, or you can journal your impressions as you read through the meditation.

This exercise encourages you to get a wider view of your life by bringing you into the future and imagining the person you want to become. As you imagine this future, make sure you allow your imagination to fly. Don't hold back. Imagine the most glorious version of yourself you possibly can.

There are some people who live in a dream world,
and there are some who face reality; and then there
are those who turn one into the other.
—Douglas H. Everett

PRACTICE

- Imagine yourself in the future, many years in the future.
- You are much older, wiser, and you're looking back upon your life.
- As you look back upon your life, you realize that all your dreams have come true; everything you wanted to happen has happened.
- As you look back upon this magnificent life, what did you do?
- What did you accomplish?
- What great adventures did you have?
- Who did you spend your time with?
- Imagine all the amazing times you had in your life from the vantage point of the much older you. See what you see; hear what you hear.
- And as you sit there imagining your much older future self, allow that future self to thank the current you for doing all the things you needed to do to enable your future self to look back upon that masterpiece of a life.
- Coming back to the present you: send love to that future version of you and reassure them that you will, indeed, take all the actions you need to take, learn all the things you need to learn, create all the habits you need to create to make this vision a reality.
- Remember that future you throughout your days, weeks, months, and years and keep that ideal you as an inspiration any time you feel like you are not moving forward. Let your wiser, older future-self guide your actions today and every day. One day, you will be that version of yourself, looking back, sending love to the you today who did all the hard work to make a spectacular life.

If you can dream it, you can do it.
—Walt Disney

BRINGING AN IDEAL SELF PRACTICE INTO YOUR LIFE

Allow yourself the freedom to daydream about what your ideal self would look like. You can do this when you are sitting at a traffic light, when you are driving, right before bed, or first thing in the morning as part of your snooze session practice. You can do this right before each meal or when you are brushing your teeth. Another idea is to set alarms throughout the day and when they go off, take a minute to dream your ideal self, your ideal life. The more you do it, the better. Keep your brain focused on the you that you dream of being and the life you dream of having and allow the magic to happen. Remember, by keeping your brain focused on the things you want to have rather than on the things you don't want to have, your brain will scan your surroundings constantly, helping you create the dream life you imagine.

What is not started today is never finished tomorrow.
—Johann Wolfgang von Goethe

REFLECT

1. What are the ways you are holding yourself back from living the best life you possibly can? Journal about this.
2. What were your hopes and dreams as a child? What were the hobbies you liked, the sports you played, the activities you did? These are clues you can use to revive these interests in your current life.

You are never too old to set another goal
or to dream a new dream.
—Les Brown

Nothing happens unless first a dream.

—CARL SANDBURG

CHAPTER 14

STACKING HABITS-BRINGING IT ALL TOGETHER

I have learned that champions aren't just born;
champions can be made when they embrace and
commit to life-changing positive habits.
—Lewis Howes

HABIT STACKING SUCCESS

I discovered habit stacking years ago when I was learning about peak per-formance. I was intrigued to learn that top performers created routines and habits that helped them live in flow. I set out to create my own routines. I started with the practices you are reading about in this book. I started out with a short meditation practice and then added a breathwork practice, then a short yoga flow. I kept adding on until I had created a full one-hour morning routine. I loved it because I was starting my day feeling good, and it made me feel like I had already won the day.

My morning Snooze Button Session changed my life. It was so great that I decided to do the same thing around my bedtime routine. Now, I have a full power hour in the morning and a power down hour in the evening. It's so beautiful to begin and end the day with these simple self-care practices. I feel like these practices have become a part of me. Eventually I added even more practices to my day, weaving them in whenever I had a few minutes. These practices have been so impactful in my life, creating such a flow and ease to my days that I decided to write **Simple Routines for Extraordinary Living,** *t**he second book in the* **Simple Tools for Extraordinary Living** *series. As I wrap up this book, I am looking forward to beginning that one.*

As I think about all the ways that the simple act of stacking one small habit on top of the other has had on my life, I am amazed. I am more productive, more focused, happier, and I feel like my life is getting better every single day. I know that you will have the same experience if you continue with these practices.

Let me say it now, *Congratulations!* You made it through the book! Great job. You are well on your way to creating a truly extraordinary life. Simple changes, done repeatedly over time, create a ripple effect and can lead to massive changes in your life. They might even totally change your life. That is why the Snooze Button Session is so effective. It is something you do every single morning, setting the tone for the day by doing something that nourishes you.

At this point, you should have at least one practice that you feel motivated about, one practice that you can continue to incorporate into your mornings. If you haven't done that, then stop for a moment to think about all the different practices we went through and ask yourself which one made you feel really good? Which one made you excited to jump out of bed? Was it meditation or breathwork? Journaling or lofty questions? Maybe movement or dancing in the morning? Whichever one it was, make sure that you continue this practice every single morning.

You now have one Snooze-Button-length morning routine which is a fantastic start.

The next step is to add on to your morning routine by committing to hitting the Snooze Button not just one time but at least two times each morning. Each time you hit the snooze button, do one of the practices you learned in this book. Since you have already built in the Snooze Button Session and practiced it for a few weeks, it is easy to use this habit as a base to stack other habits onto. This is a practice called habit stacking. Habit stacking is when you take something you already do and add on to that built in habit.

The Snooze Button technique utilizes habit stacking by taking something you already do, hitting the Snooze Button, and adding on something you want to do like meditating. Adding on a second Snooze Button Session is simple now that you know the technique. Who knows, you might even go a step further and commit to setting your alarm even earlier than usual so that you can do multiple Snooze Button Sessions. Simply determine how many practices you want to add to your day and then multiply that by the number of minutes between your alarms. Set your alarm that amount of time earlier and there you have it. A full morning routine.

The easiest way to create the extraordinary life you imagine is to regularly practice new positive habits. Installing a morning routine will help you move in this direction without much effort or work on your part. You will notice that you start to feel better and better as you continue your morning routine, slowly adding to it until you have a sustainable, uplifting morning practice that makes you feel great.

The most difficult part of creating change in your life is to install the new positive habits that you need. Taking something you are already doing, like brushing your teeth, and stacking another habit right on top of it, makes it a lot easier to remember to do the new habit. Brushing your teeth is something that you are trained to do since you do it every day. The neural connections are strong. Stacking another habit on top of this one makes it simple to remember and easy to accomplish. Soon enough, the new habit becomes just as easy to do as the original habit. That is the beauty of habit stacking.

IDEAS FOR HABIT STACKING

There are many opportunities throughout the day that you can incorporate habit stacking. Take any regular habit you have like brushing your teeth, eating your meals, getting into your car, or driving to work and then add on to it. Take a new habit you want to implement and use the already established habit to help you create the new habit. Make a list of all the regular habits you have and use them as opportunities to add a positive change to your day. Take some time to think about what you could do to add a sense of peace and calm throughout your day and then implement it.

Habit Stacking Throughout the Day:
- Silently repeat your affirmations or lofty questions to yourself as you brush your teeth in the morning.
- Think about what you are grateful for when you brush your teeth at night.
- Take a walk every day after lunch.
- Spend five minutes listening to music in your car before or after your work day.
- Take a moment to forgive someone each morning after breakfast.
- Meditate or do breathwork for a few minutes every time you feel the urge to go on social media.
- While you are sitting at a traffic light, envision your dream life.
- Tell yourself you love yourself each morning.
- Every time you walk through a doorway, think about someone you are grateful for.
- Every time you leave your house, do three relaxation breaths.

- Anytime you get into your car, notice something beautiful around you.
- Each night before you fall asleep, journal about all the amazing things you witnessed that day.

Motivation is what gets you started.
Habit is what keeps you going.
—Jim Rohn

If you are going to achieve excellence in big things, you develop the habit in little matters. Excellence is not an exception, it is a prevailing attitude.

—COLIN POWELL

CHAPTER 15

BRINGING THE PRACTICES INTO YOUR DAY

If you pick the right small behavior and sequence it right,
then you won't have to motivate yourself to have it grow.
It will just happen naturally, like a good seed
planted in a good spot.
—BJ Fogg

MAKING IT A LIFESTYLE

When I became a yoga teacher, I realized yoga is not just a series of poses, instead, it is a lifestyle, a way of being in the world. I was intrigued with this idea, and I set out to live this lifestyle. I began to look at everything as a chance to practice peace and calm. Doing laundry, cooking, cleaning—these all became meditations.

I began to listen to audio books or uplifting content anytime I was in the car. When I was waiting for my kids to finish an activity, I had a book *in the car to read while I waited or I would take those minutes to get out and walk around, to let the sun warm my face. Instead of waiting to live, I began to live every moment, and I have found this to be a beautiful way to go through life.*

I created morning routines, evening routines and other routines that I implemented throughout my day. My entire life changed and I was so enthusiastic about the process that I kept detailed notes on my unfolding journey. I eventually began to teach these routines and my students reported that their lives were changing too. The Snooze Button Sessions is the first book in the series detailing these routines that changed my life. It is my hope they change your life as well.

Start here, with this book and once you have your morning routine down, move on to the other books in this series. Please reach out to me to tell me how these practices affect your life. I would love to hear from you on Instagram @iamkerryfisher or on my website kerryfishercoaching.com. If we are ever to meet, I would love to hear about your wins and we shall celebrate together. I look forward to that day.

Ok guys, this is where the pedal hits the metal. This is where we supercharge the practices you have learned throughout this book. This is where the true change happens, and your entire life becomes a masterpiece.

You learned many different techniques that will increase your calm, your focus, your sense of peace, while decreasing your stress, anxiety, and overwhelm. You have also learned that you can stack these practices onto existing habits like brushing your teeth or eating a meal, so they are easier to implement. Now it's time to look for opportunities throughout the day where you are under-utilizing your time and use those times as opportunities to do something that makes you feel great. Here's where the true magic happens.

Bring these practices into your day as many times and in as many ways as you can. Find times throughout the day where you can do one of the techniques you learned in this book. You can add a short meditation session during your workday or after a stressful meeting. You can practice your breathing exercises while in line at a store. You can take a walk after work each day. Schedule in these extra times that you will be practicing the techniques you learned in this book. Or maybe, there are other things that you want to add to your day that were not in this book.

There are so many times during the day that you have pockets of time. Using this time to make yourself feel good is so much better than using it to scroll or browse social media feeds. Remember, we want to increase the things that feel good and reduce the things that feel bad. That's the way to truly change. Find that time throughout your day! The irony is that filling these small gaps of time—standing in line, driving to work, waiting for your kids—with positive new thoughts and activities does not take more energy away from you. Rather, filling these gaps with positive thoughts and activities actually invigorates you, providing you with more energy to handle your daily tasks.

IDEAS FOR BRINGING PRACTICES INTO YOUR DAY

This chapter is about bringing the practices into your day. So take some time to journal and figure out when you can carve out more time from your day to do the things that make you feel good.

These days, we have endless options for how we can spend our free moments. All too often, we spend those precious moments gazing at a screen, reading the news or browsing social media. Get really serious with yourself. Do you really feel good after doing that?

I'm going to get super real here. Be *honest* with yourself. How is your life going? Is your life a masterpiece? Do you want it to be? If so, it's time to roll up your sleeves and get to work. Begin small like we have suggested by creating your morning routine, but don't stop there, keep going. Find moments in your day where you can claw back time and instead of gazing into a screen, use that time to take care of your body, mind, and spirit.

So how do you go about bringing these practices into your day? Simply find a few practices that you really enjoy and then find some time during your day to do them. Remember what I talked about when I said you can "claw back" time? Sit and make a list of the times you would normally be waiting or when you would typically watch TV or use your phone or computer and start doing these practices instead.

Remember, it's a practice. So take your time. Practice. Add a little bit at a time. In the same way you found the time to create a morning routine, you can begin to slowly add these amazing, nourishing techniques into your life. Remember to do the ones that make you really happy. The more joyful you are when you are doing any of these activities, the more likely you will want to add more of them into your life. Before you know it, you will no longer need to practice because you will be living it.

Here are a few ideas of when you can practice these techniques:

- During your commute
- When you are waiting to pick up your kids
- Right before work if you get there early
- Directly after work, before you head home
- During your lunch break
- In a doctor's waiting room
- Waiting in line at the store
- Anytime you are about to pull out your phone

If you're serious about changing your life, you'll find a way.
If you're not, you'll find an excuse.
—Jen Sincero

You define your own life. Don't let other people write your script.

—OPRAH WINFREY

CHAPTER 16

FINAL WORDS

This is not a goodbye, my darling, this is a thank you.
—Nicholas Sparks

The practices in this book can and will change your life if you allow them to. The first step is to simply begin. Go easy on yourself. According to Phillippa Lally et al in *European Journal of Social Psychology*, it can take as little as 66 days to install a new habit. It's ok if you start and stop at first. Just pick it back up if you notice you stopped, do not get upset with yourself.

So how do you start? You just have to do it. You just have to start. I remember we used to have family meetings, and we would introduce something we wanted our kids to change. We would ask them, how are you going to change this behavior? Each of my children would inevitably say, "I'll just stop." It was funny and became a standing joke because they very rarely stopped the behavior just because they said they would stop. But the behavior would start to change over time, and I realized it was because of repetition. It was as if they instilled a reminder within themselves that this behavior needed to be altered. The reminder would seep into their minds. Eventually, the change did indeed occur. The same is true with trying to instill new habits. We need to stop procrastinating and JUST START!

Start immediately and practice regularly. Eventually the new habit will feel natural, and you will notice positive changes in your life.

I've been teaching these techniques to my students for years. The idea behind what I teach is: you can create massive change in your life. You can have massive shifts by simply installing small changes slowly over time. Although it would be great to just wake up one day and have all these healthy habits in place, that is not the way it works. Most adults have very busy lives so trying to make massive changes immediately typically leads to failure.

Take New Year's Resolutions for instance—we make all these resolutions that we will work out, eat right, be patient with kids, spend more time outdoors, become more serious about our career, and improve our relationships. We make these resolutions at the end of the year when we are feeling great from the holidays and looking forward to a fresh start in the new year. The new year arrives, and with the best of intentions we begin to try to stick with our resolutions. But beginning on New Year's Day may seem unrealistic, of course, because we are tired. And the day after New Year's, we're too busy trying to get back into our routine. Finally, we start to focus on our resolutions and valiantly try to incorporate them into our life. We typically succeed for a few days, until inevitably, we skip a day. One day turns into two. Then, before we know it, the resolutions are a distant memory. We basically set ourselves up for failure.

The way the brain works isn't to decide to make huge changes and everything is perfect. Rather what happens is that each time we get a little success in something, we get a little hit of dopamine, the feel-good chemical. This drives us to try to succeed again, so we can get another hit of dopamine.

Each morning when the alarm sounds, and you do one of the practices from this book, you will get that sense of satisfaction and those feel-good chemicals flood into your body. By starting your day this way, you are putting yourself into a really positive space to create an amazing day.

The beauty of the simple tools in the Snooze Button Sessions system is that they allow you to have a sense of ease as you create change in your life. You are moving step by step, snooze by snooze, towards the next grandest version of yourself. Be bold. Be audacious. Be strong. Be brave. Do all the things you dream of doing be all the things you dream of being. Share your gifts with the world. There is only one you, and your gifts are meant to be expressed.

You only have this one life. Make it a great one

> *Don't die with the music still inside you.*
> —Wayne Dyer

It is my sincerest hope that you will take these practices into your life and create the very best life you can possibly imagine. In light of that, I want to share this True Purpose Meditation with you. This passage originally appeared in my very first foray into the world of publishing in a chapter I wrote for the book *Winning Mindset* by Erik Seversen et. al. Check out kerryfishercoaching.com for a link to the True Purpose Meditation made especially for this book. Enjoy!

TRUE PURPOSE MEDITATION: MY LOVE LETTER TO YOU

You can live the life of your dreams. You can be the person you dream of being. You can. Did you hear that?

Let me say that again. I want you to really take this in. Take a deep breath in and a long breath out through your mouth.

You can live the life of your dreams. You can be the person you dream of being. And you will. You will.

You are here for a reason. You are here to be all the things you dream of being. To do all the things you dream of doing.

It's time to throw off your chains. Today is the day. You were born for a reason. You are here for a purpose. You know it. You feel it. But you doubt it.

Why is that? Well, this is why: you were trained to doubt this, trained to doubt yourself, trained to discard what you knew in your heart so you could fit into the group.

No more. Starting today, you turn a new chapter. You become the person you know you are deep in your soul.

Let me tell you a little story: when you were born, you knew exactly who you were. You knew exactly why you were here. You were born perfect in every way.

Babies are pure and blissful. They live fully in the moment. They can lay and stare at their hand and be endlessly amazed at it. They know wonder. They know joy. They don't worry about what is going to happen next week or next year. They fully exist in the moment. They know who they are, and they are happy to be who they are.

They aren't trying to change. They don't think...gee, if only I had a different color hair or different color eyes. A better brand of diaper. A nicer crib. No, they are happy with who they are. Because they know who they are. They know why they are here. They are here to live, to experience all that life has to offer. To express the fullest version of who they are.

They laugh when they are happy and cry when they are sad. They aren't scared to try new things. They don't lay there thinking...hmmm, I would love to crawl but what if I fail? No. Instead, they try to crawl and fail, try to crawl and fail and then eventually, they learn to crawl. And then walk. And then run. They don't give up. They don't get upset with themselves when they can't do it right away. Instead, they practice and fail, practice and fail, practice and fail. Until they succeed. Right?

And then what happens?

The baby grows up. People start to tell them they can't do this; they can't do that. Their parents, teachers, family, friends, everyone telling them what they can and cannot do. Telling them who they should and should not be.

Gradually, the veils fall down, the mask slips on. The true self gets hidden. They assume a false identity, live a life they didn't really want. Live by rules made by others. They lose who they are to become who everyone else wants them to be.

You know what I'm saying. You can feel truth when it hits you. We all can. So I am here to tell you this. It is time to drop the mask. To uncover who you really are. Because you are here for a reason.

You can live the life of your dreams. You can have it all. You can be the person you have always dreamed of being. Let's start now.

You see things; and you say, 'Why?'
But I dream things that never were; and I say, 'Why not?'
—George Bernard Shaw

*What we call the beginning
is often the end.
And to make an end is to
make a beginning.
The end is where we start from.*

—T.S. ELIOT

A MESSAGE FROM KERRY

I have been doing the practices in this book for many years, and they truly have changed my life. I feel better, and I look better. I am kinder, nicer, and calmer. Beginning my day by nurturing myself and taking time for me has been a true game changer. Is my life perfect? Of course not. There are many areas in my life I'm still working on. My goal is not perfection. My goal is to simply get a little bit better every single day.

A few years ago, I decided to live my purpose and to do everything I needed to do to get there. Writing this book is the culmination of that journey for me and completing this book serves as a massive impetus for me to continue writing and sharing my learnings with you. I have felt a sense of purpose the entire time I wrote the book, feeling a sense of rightness and inevitability that this is the book I was meant to write, that the readers who found this book were the people I was meant to reach. It means so much to me that you read it and from the bottom of my heart, I thank you.

I hope this book has been valuable to you, and I hope that each morning, when your alarm rings, you jump up joyously to practice something that makes you feel truly alive. I hope these practices fuel your day. I want to share with you that there were lots of bumps and obstacles on the path to getting this book finished. First, I wrote half of it and left it sitting in my computer for over a year. Then, I shared it with a dear friend and we decided to collaborate to bring the book into the world. This was followed by six months of joyous collaboration as we each decided which chapters we would write and then wrote them. We were in the flow. The book was finally complete, and I rejoiced until my collaborator and I had a parting of ways. Within the span of a week, I went from having a fully completed manuscript to a half-done manuscript.

It felt like a lot of work to rewrite half the book, but the calling of my soul kept pushing me, so I wrote. And I loved it. I rewrote all of the chapters I needed to rewrite but in the process, I also rewrote a lot of the chapters I had previously written, adding details that I had not included when I first wrote my chapters. The manuscript took on a life of its own, and it felt like I was channeling the book, not writing it. It was coming through me, not from me. It was such an incredible experience.

As I write this, I feel a sense of joy and excitement. I have a huge sense of accomplishment as I write these final words. My dream has come true, in large part thanks to my decision all those years ago to hit my snooze button and meditate. I think back from the vantage point of this moment, all the way back to when I first hit the snooze button and see how that moment truly led to this. I am a living example of how the Snooze Button Sessions really do work.

Thank you for coming on this journey with me by reading this book. It is my mission in life to live the best life I can possibly live and to help others do the same. This book is a huge step towards fulfilling my mission.

My wish for you is that you become the very best version of yourself, and you live the very best life you can live.

From my heart to yours, I send you love, light, and laughter.

XO Kerry

ACKNOWLEDGEMENTS

From my earliest memories I had a dream of having lots of children, a loving husband, a house filled with animals, activity and a bit of chaos. I have been lucky that my dream has come true thanks to my husband Keith and my kids.

Tyler, you made me a mother and taught me what it meant to be responsible for someone besides myself. I remember how amazed I was by everything about you. Your tiny hands, your tiny feet. It was so lovely to watch you grow into the man you are today. Smart, funny and endlessly curious, you have always been someone I admire.

Kolby, I was so happy to welcome you into the world. You made Tyler a big brother and the two of you were best friends back then. I remember being in awe of your insight, your ability to see right through people. You had an incredible ability to see past the surface to who a person really is. You have always had a spectacular smile and a love of how things work. Most impressive to me though is your sense of self. You were always true to who you are, very self assured in what you wanted and determined to live exactly how you wanted to live. It is something I really look up to and makes me proud to be your mother.

Tyler and Kolby, those early years of motherhood are amongst my favorite memories. You enabled me to see the beauty of the world around me through your eyes. Those years were the innocent easy years. We boldly explored together and life was sweet.

Tanner, you came along exactly when we needed you most. With an easy smile and a ready laugh, you were so easy to take care of. You were carefree and silly, always making funny faces and entertaining us. Your relaxed attitude towards life is such a lesson to me. I love who you are and how open and honest you have always been with me. I admire you so much.

Skye when you came along, I was able to experience what it was like to have a little girl. When I was pregnant with you, everyone asked me if I wanted a girl and I would say, "No, I just want a healthy baby." When you were born, though, I realized that I had wanted a girl without even realizing. You brought color , glitter and fun into my life. I always think of you as a glam tomboy, wearing your glittery shoes, your pink dress but climbing a tree. You were born knowing exactly who you are. Strong, independent and headstrong, you taught me the meaning of fierce and fearless. I am so proud of the woman you are becoming.

And Chase. An old soul who is sensitive, sweet and kind. You think so deeply about things and feel things so strongly and it is truly a beautiful quality. You balance that out by being very independent and strong willed. Nobody has ever been able to tell you what to do and I know this quality will be a great one for you as you go out into the world. I am so happy we have such a close bond. I respect your tenacity, your dedication and the way you always hug Dad and I every single time we leave the house. You taught us the meaning of unconditional love.

I love all of you so much. Being your mom has always been and will always be the most important job to me. I know I haven't always been the mom you wanted but I hope you all know how much I love you and admire you and respect you.

Keith, we have been together more than half of our lifetimes. When I think back upon all the years, I see there were moments when we fell to our knees and there were moments when we reached the highest heights. Through it all you have been steady, at my side, grounding me and rooting me to the earth. You are always there for me, you always encourage me to live my biggest dreams and I appreciate you for that. I think the thing I appreciate about you most, though, is that you allow me to be exactly who I am. Thank you for being at my side all these years. I know it hasn't always been easy.

To my mom and step dad Barry, thank you for always supporting me and encouraging me to strive ever higher. Michele, our bond is unbreakable and you really are a great sister. We have had so many ridiculous times together and through it all we laughed, laughed, laughed. Bryan and Sharn, you may technically my brothers in law, but in my heart you are my full brothers. Zach, Dylan, Logan, Hayden, Garrett and Remy, I love you guys, thanks for being the coolest nephews ever.

To all my students past and future, thank you for trusting me and helping me grow into the very best version of myself. It is because of you that I continually learn and grow, morph and change.

And to you, dear readers, I thank you. I have held the dream of being a published author in my heart since I was a little girl and it is you I thought about as I wrote this book. Thank you for your support.

XO Kerry

Life is but a dream, within a dream.
—Shakespeare

FOR FURTHER INFORMATION

Thank you for reading this book. It is my hope that you received a lot of value from the material presented here. It is my hope that this book will help you become the next greatest version of yourself so that you can live your most extraordinary life.

The books in the extraordinary life series offer tips, techniques, routines, practices and exercises for living your dream life.

If you enjoyed this book, please leave a review on the site where you purchased the book. Please share this book with anyone who you think could benefit from the information in this book.

For more information and to access the
resources in this book, please go to:

kerryfishercoaching.com

where you will find all the video resources
mentioned within the book.

You can also follow Kerry on Instagram:
@iamkerryfisher .

LOOK FOR OTHER BOOKS BY THE AUTHOR

THE EXTRAORDINARY LIVING SERIES:

The Extraordinary Living Series is a series of books with one central premise. You can live the life of your dreams, you can become the person you dream of becoming. All it takes is action. The series teaches you the tools, techniques and tips that will help you take control of your life so that you can create the masterpiece life you have always imagined.

ROUTINES FOR EXTRAORDINARY LIVING

The second book in the extraordinary living series, *Routines for Extraordinary Living* is for those people who want to create change in their life but don't know where to start. The book takes you step by step through your day, teaching you how to establish nourishing routines throughout the day to move you towards the extraordinary life you deserve. This book is all about creating a lifestyle where healthy routines are woven into your day. You will create practices that are built into your everyday life that nourish your body, your mind and your spirit. Before you know it, your life will be one of ease and flow which enables you to have the energy you need to create the life you desire.

PEAK PERFORMANCE FOR EXTRAORDINARY LIVING

The third book in the extraordinary living series, *Peak Performance for Extraordinary Living* is for people who are ready to take their lives to the next level. The book goes deep into the science behind why we do what we do. You will learn about the way your brain and your nervous system work and how you can use your biology to create the life you have dreamed of. You will learn how to make goals that align with your true purpose here on earth and then you will create the plan to make those goals a reality. This book examines the way our emotions work, how our nervous system and brain seek to protect us, and gives you the tools you need to rewire your brain so that you can create the masterpiece of a life that you deserve.

INSIGHTS FOR EXTRAORDINARY LIVING

One of Kerry's deepest wishes from a very young age was to be a writer. It was a secret dream she rarely shared with anyone.

On January 2, 2022, Kerry was sitting in her backyard reading The Alchemist by Paulo Coelho. The book is about a shepherd boy who was on a quest to find his life's purpose. As Kerry read the book, she asked herself one simple question, "What is my life's purpose?" She was surprised when the thought immediately jumped into her head, "You are here to write."

The next thought was this, "What does a writer do?"

The answer again jumped into her head, "A writer writes."

And as the sun rose over the horizon, on the second day of 2022, Kerry made a decision that she would write every day for an entire year. She decided to write on a platform called Insights by Mindvalley and each day for a full year, she wrote an insight. She didn't miss a day. The daily writing fueled her passion for writing. She decided to write a book on the tools she had discovered that helped her lead a great ife and the Extraordinary Living series came to life.

One day, a friend told Kerry how much she had been enjoying Kerry's daily insights. She suggested that she publish them as an anthology. Over the next week, three other people said the same thing to her. And so, Kerry began the process of reading through her year of daily insights. She envisioned a new series, based on these simple stories of self reflection and deep soul searching.

The Insights series is a powerful reminder that every single person we meet is our teacher, and every single event in our life can serve as a lesson. They remind you that you can become the person you dream of becoming, you can live the extraordinary life you imagine. It just takes an inquisitive mind and an open heart. Check out the series and see what insights they bring for you.

BREATHWORK FOR EXTRAORDINARY LIVING

A deep dive into the breath. The mystics have been practicing breath exercises for thousands of years. They found that doing these breath exercises helped them get to deeper levels of meditation. The yogis have known the power of the breath as well. So have many of the Eastern traditions. The exciting thing is that science is now catching up with the wisdom of the ages. Recent studies have shown how powerful a breath practice can be in creating new states within your body. Indeed, the studies indicate that breath is an incredible tool we can use to help balance our emotions and our mental state. If you want to learn simple breath tools you can use to help you live a life of balance and ease, look for this wonderful book.

MEDITATION FOR EXTRAORDINARY LIVING

Meditation has long been used by many religious and spiritual traditions to tap into altered states of mind. The mystics from the ages used meditation to help them to move into deep states of awareness and consciousness. They found that meditation kept them calm in body, mind and spirit. Meditation has become increasingly common across the world because it is one of the best ways to change your state of being. This book will teach you many different meditation techniques so you can bring this practice into your life.

BREATHWORK FOR EXTRAORDINARY LIVING

Breathwork is an amazing practice that has been used by many spirited calming breath practices that helped them to tap into single minded focus and balance their emotions. They also developed breath practices that would warm their bodies and get them ready for action. The exciting thing is that science now proves that the benefits of a breath practice are immense. Indeed, breath practice is known to change your state instantly, Check out this book to learn all about the breath so you can incorporate this powerful practice into your life.

BE EXTRAORDINARY PUBLISHING

Check out all the books under the Be Extraordinary imprint. Our mission is to show you how to be the very best version of yourself, how to live the very best life you can possibly live. Our books are all about bringing attention to all the important areas of your life so that you can uplevel them all.

We publish books on a variety of health and wellness topics as well as on peak performance and mindset. We focus on personal transformation and teach you how you can live your best life. Look for books on a wide variety of topics including nutrition, exercise, yoga, pilates, meditation, breathwork, mindfulness practices, and self care. Our books will show you how you can upgrade your life using simple techniques, tips and tricks to create a magnificent life.

We also bring you stories of the heroes amongst us. Stories of the journey towards extraordinary living. These books illuminate how every person is on a Hero's Journey, how every person is on a journey towards extraordinary. Look for our books on Amazon, in bookstores and everywhere books are sold.

Routines for Extraordinary Living

A GUIDE FOR LIVING YOUR BEST LIFE

BOOK II IN THE EXTRAORDINARY LIVING SERIES

*The secret of getting ahead
is getting started.
The secret of getting started
is breaking your complex,
overwhelming tasks into
small, manageable tasks,
and then starting on the first one.*

—MARK TWAIN

INTRODUCTION

THE SECRET TO LIFE

You are never too old to set another goal
or to dream a new dream.
—C. S. Lewis

H ere is the secret to life: YOU are the person creating your life. Only you.

Have you ever thought of it this way before? That you are the only person who has created the life you are living?

Now you might be thinking...no, I didn't create this life. I'm not able to control everything around me. I didn't control where I was born, who my family was, my upbringing, the people I met in my life, the situations that happened to me.

This is what many people believe. They believe that they were not the ones who created their life, that they had a lot of trauma and drama thrown at them and they did the best they could under the circumstances.

I don't mean to burst your bubble. But here's one simple fact: YOU have created every single thing in your life. Only you.

To be more precise, your choices have created the person that you are, the life you lead.

You might be resisting this idea. It's so much easier to blame your parents, spouse, children, or boss for what is going on in your life. It's hard to take full and total responsibility for the idea that it was actually you that created the reality that you are living in. Especially if your life feels like it's a mess.

But it's true. You created every single thing around you by your thoughts, words and deeds. It was YOUR actions that created your life.

Here's the good news, though. Since you are the one who created your life, you are also the one who can create a different life. A better life. The life of your dreams. Imagine that!

Before we go any further, stop and take a look at your life. Look at the people in your life, the circumstances of your life, your home, your career, your family. You were the one that created all the things as they are. You are the one that created the relationships the way they are, you are the one that created your home, your career, your life. All that you see is the result of the choices you made. And the choices you made were the result of the way that you think, your mindset.

If your life is not the way that you want it to be, it is because you have never truly examined what you really want, who you really are. In order to create your life, you need to know exactly what you want, exactly who you are and exactly who you want to become. Even more important, you need to look at your beliefs and see what you are thinking about yourself and about your life. You need to see if there are limiting beliefs that are stopping you from creating the life you dream of.

Consider this, if your life were a movie, would you be the main character or a bit player? Would the movie of your life be a drama, a comedy, an inspirational masterpiece? Even more importantly, in the movie that is your life, do you want to be the main character or a bit player? Do you want to live a drama, a comedy or an inspirational masterpiece?

If you want to live an inspirational masterpiece, then this book will help you get there. If you want to keep living in drama and trauma, put this book down, grab some ice cream, go sit on the couch and watch tv all day.

This book is all about action. Massive action. Massive action towards the life of your dreams, the life you have until now, only imagined, This book is not for someone who wants to sit passively as life passes them by. Instead, it is for people who are ready, willing and able to make a change. If you install the routines detailed in this book, your life will change. So get ready. You are about to supercharge your life.

Twenty years from now you'll be more disappointed
by the things you did not do
than the ones you did.
—Mark Twain

MY STORY

It's always good to know who is guiding you on your journey so let me tell you a little bit about me. I am a mom of 5. I have been, at various points of my life: a lawyer, a stay at home mom, a yoga teacher, a meditation teacher, and a mindset coach for athletes. I have fulfilled my dreams of becoming a published author and I am pursuing a new goal now, becoming an international speaker. It has been a long journey to this life I am currently leading today.

My life began to change drastically when I turned 50. I had an epiphany during a family vacation where I realized that although I had accomplished everything I had set out to accomplish, I wasn't happy.

I decided to write a list of all the goals I wanted to accomplish, all the adventures I wanted to have, all the ways I wanted to change my life. As I looked at this comprehensive list of goals and dreams, I wondered how I could ever make any of those things come true.

One day, when my alarm went off, I hit the Snooze Button but instead of going back to sleep, I meditated. When the alarm went off once more, I got up and went about my day. That evening I was thinking back upon my day and I realized the day had gone really smoothly. I told my husband about it and he asked me what I had done differently and I remembered my morning meditation. I told him about it and the next morning he woke up with me, we hit the Snooze Button and meditated, At the end of the day, he told me that his day had been smooth and stress free,

We both continued using our morning Snooze Button Sessions to meditate. Eventually, I added on, hitting the Snooze Button multiple times and before I knew it, I had a 1 hour morning routine where I meditated, did breathwork, practiced yoga, listened to music, and journaled. I was waking up an hour earlier than usual but somehow I had more energy and I felt great. I was teaching yoga at the time so I started to teach this technique to my students and they reported incredible results.

I had created a way to take action, to actually incorporate the healthy habits that we all need to have a balanced life. I dubbed this technique the Snooze Button Sessions and taught it to everyone I knew. My morning Snooze Button Sessions helped me move in a positive direction towards a new way of living and soon enough, it would change the direction of my life.

One morning, as I was journaling, I wrote down that I wanted to be a New York TImes bestselling author. As I wrote it, I knew that it was my deepest heart's desire, something I had thought about my entire life. At that moment, I made the decision to begin. But what would I write about? Instantly the answer popped into my head. I would write about the morning Snooze Button Sessions.

Before I knew it, I was using some of the time in the morning to actually write my first book, *Simple TIps for Extraordinary Living:The Snooze Button Sessions*. My morning sessions had helped me to write a book on my morning sessions! It was fantastic and opened my eyes to the idea that maybe, just maybe, I could have a career as an author as I had always dreamed.

Start where you are.
Use what you have. Do what you can.
—Arthur Ashe

And then, a few years later, on a family trip (those family trips are real eye openers, I seem to have all my aha moments there), I had another epiphany. This one was more painful than the first one. You see, during this trip, I realized that all the things I thought about the family I had worked so hard to build, all the things I thought about my relationships with my children and my husband, all the things I thought about the life I had built were not true. It was a dark moment of the soul moment for me when I had this moment of clarity.

During the months after that trip, I had to face a lot of uncomfortable truths about myself, about my life, about my relationships. About everything. It was a time of deep reflection for me. It was very painful because I felt like I had spent a quarter of a century pouring my love and caring into my family & they didn't even care about me. I kept thinking that after all my effort, all my hard work, all I had sacrificed, there was no reciprocity, no love. I was not appreciated or respected by those I loved the most.

I felt unloved but more than that, I felt unworthy of love, unworthy of affection, unworthy of respect. I felt terrible about myself. I resolved to take an even deeper dive inward and what I found was not pretty. I did a lot of work on myself and I came to understand that I had been trying to find my value and self worth through my family. I understood that all the years of caretaking and sacrifice had been my way of trying to get love and affection and acceptance. I was shaken to my core as I realized that everything I believed was based on this quest for love.

I also realized that I had been acting like a victim. And nobody likes a victim, especially me.

The moment I realized that I had been acting like a victim, I took action. I decided to overhaul my entire life by becoming very clear on the kind of life I wanted to create. That was the moment that I found a program called Lifebook. Lifebook is an elegant system created by Jon and Missy Butcher where you think deeply about 12 areas of your life.

I took the course and thought deeply about my health and fitness, my intellectual life, my emotional and spiritual life. I examined my philosophy on my social life and my relationships. I thought about my dream career and how I wanted my financial life to be. Finally, I thought about my quality of life and my life vision.

Up until LIfebook, I had never examined each of these areas of my life in such detail. As a matter of fact, there were some areas I had never examined at all. I also learned that the areas where I had thought I was doing great were actually the areas that I needed to do the most work in.

In the end, I created a 200 page book about what I think about my philosophy in each category of life, what my vision for that area was and a strategy for that area.

I loved looking at my personalized book holding all my hopes and dreams. It was eye opening. What I didn't know at the time was that this book would open the door to a whole new life for me.

I now had a clear vision of where I wanted to go.

A few months passed. I lost the book in my house. The global pandemic came and shut down the world. A few more months passed. It was winter now, I was cleaning out a closet and found my lifebook. As I leafed through it, I was shocked. So many of the things had come true.

I had finished writing my first book and was in the process of editing it. I had become more active with fun outdoor activities and my children had too. I had like minded friends from around the world. Somehow, by magic, it had happened, I had been moving towards the life of my dreams without even realizing it.

As I thought about how this had happened, I knew, absolutely knew, it was because I had gotten crystal clear clarity on what I wanted, I had taken action. I had taken massive action. Each and every day, I had taken action. Some days I had made massive progress and others I had taken small steps but I had taken action every single day.

I had installed routines and habits that helped me become healthier, happier and more productive. That was why my life had changed. This book is a compilation of the techniques I used to change my life. It worked for me and it can work for you.

Small deeds done are better than great deeds planned.
—Peter Marshall

WHAT YOU WILL LEARN

This book will show you how I installed simple routines into my daily life, little by little, and how those routines changed my life. My philosophy is that you can create massive change by using simple tools, you can take simple steps, improving bit by bit and eventually that will change your life.

In my previous book, *The Snooze Sessions*, I shared simple tools that you could immediately incorporate into your mornings in order to witness noticeable improvements in your life.

Either you run the day or the day runs you.
—Jim Rohn

In this book, I expand on this idea by demonstrating how you can install amazing routines throughout your day and create the levels of energy, the abundant health, the rewarding relationships that enable you to create the life of your dreams. It has been said that the way you do one thing is the way you do everything. That is why these simple routines will create the positive change you need to change your life. Your decisions, your daily habits, your thoughts, words, actions create your reality.

How do you start? Radical responsibility. You have to take complete and utter responsibility for the idea that every single thing in your life, every person, every situation, every thought, every EVERYTHING in your life was created by you. Your decisions brought you here. That's the hardest step. It can be difficult to accept that you created your entire life, even the messy parts. But once you do, everything will change.

Why does everything change? Well, here's the good news. SInce you are the one who created everything around you, that means that you can begin making different choices in order to create the life you dream of living, starting in this very moment. You can decide to live a life where you nourish your body, mind and soul every single day. Yes, you can!

You can spend time with the people you want to. You get to decide what you read, what you watch and how you spend each minute of your precious life.

This book is all about action. Creating small changes each day which eventually lead you towards a new way of living. You take action every single day, step by step, moving forward ever forward towards that life that you imagine. This book will help you to create the right habits, thoughts, words, actions to create the reality that you dream of.

As you install these positive daily routines in your life, you will begin to transform and your life will begin to transform. It's happened for me and it can happen for you. It will happen for you.

Today, you are beginning the journey towards creating a life where you jump out of bed each morning with abundant energy and joy, ready to take on the day, ready to live your extraordinary life. Let's get started. Let's create a blueprint for how to begin and end your days with intention, joy, peace, excitement and fun.

Let us begin. Let's create your dream life, the life you deserve. A life of peace, intention, joy, excitement and fun. It's your life, make it a masterpiece.

Go confidently in the direction of your dreams.
Live the life you've imagined.
—Henry David Thoreau

HOW TO USE THIS BOOK

This book is all about action.

In order to get the most out of the book, you must take action. Simply reading the book will give you some ideas and tips but if you want to see real change in a relatively short period of time, you must do the work. Do all the exercises and answer the questions.

Take your time as you work through the book. There is a lot of information here, a lot of tips, tools and techniques for installing new routines into your life. It is best to take it slow. Read the chapter, learn the concepts and then assess where you are in that area of your life. Then begin to create the routine that will work for you.

Remember that there is no right or wrong way to create these routines. There is only a right or wrong way for you. The book is predicated upon the fact that we are all different and what works for one person does not necessarily work for the next person. The book is structured so that you can learn the ideas and then tailor the routines to your life.

The book has 4 parts.

Part I is where you think about what an extraordinary life means to you. You will be doing an exercise where you will think about all the categories of your life and determine what your beliefs are about that category, what is working in what needs to be improved and why and how you can use them to create massive change in your life by making small daily choices that support the life you are moving towards.

Part II is where the pedal hits the metal. This is where you will begin to actually create the routines that will support you on your journey towards greatness. You will create a morning routine and an evening routine. You will create a list of daily actions that will help you have the energy you need to do all the amazing things you envision. By the end of Part II, you will have new routines that nourish and strengthen you. You will have taken action and will be well on your way to your extraordinary life.

Part III is all about your health and wellness. You will begin with an assessment to see where you are and then you will learn a little bit about how important hydration and nutrition is to maintain the energy levels you need. Don't worry, we aren't going too deep here, these are meant to be simple routines that you can put into action now to move in the direction of your ultimate health goals. You will also look at your activity level and begin to add some muscle endurance and cardiovascular fitness routines into your weekly schedule. The final chapter of this section focuses on adding fun, healthy activities to your life so that you can maintain your physical, mental and emotional health.

Part IV is where you will focus on creating the best quality of life you possibly can. Here you will delve into the adventures you want to have, the way you want to live in your home and your relationships. This part of the book is where you begin to make the external changes to your surroundings so that your home becomes the oasis of peace and calmness you need. You will look deeply at your relationships and begin to improve the ones you have and expand into a new way of being that supports who you are becoming. Finally, you will focus on adding fun into your life, dreaming up your own personal bucket list of adventures you want to have, trips you want to take, new hobbies and sports you want to bring into your life.

By the end of the book, you will be a completely different person. You will have a completely different life. I am rooting for you!

XO Kerry

Inaction breeds doubt and fear.
Action breeds confidence
and courage.
If you want to conquer fear, do
not sit home and think about it.
Go out and get busy.

—DALE CARNEGIE

ABOUT THE AUTHOR

Kerry was raising a family and working as an attorney when she began a daily yoga practice. She immediately noticed that yoga was the perfect antidote to her hectic lifestyle. Initially interested in yoga as a physical practice that made her feel good in her body, Kerry soon realized yoga was a lot more than that. She decided to take a teacher training and immediately began teaching. Kerry eventually left her law career and began to focus on teaching and coaching full time.

Kerry's mission is to help others find a more balanced and fulfilled life. She believes in action and has created a system that is easy to implement so that people can create change quickly. Kerry teaches Simple Tips for Extraordinary Living using stress reduction techniques and work-life balance to help people supercharge their lives. She coaches corporate clients and elite athletes in mindset and peak performance techniques and creates tailored programs for private clients who are seeking mastery in all areas of their lives.

After many years of teaching and coaching, Kerry is focused on writing, creating courses and speaking on the topics she is so passionate about. She is on a mission to inspire and encourage people to become the person they dream of being and to create the life they imagine.

When not teaching or writing, you can usually find Kerry somewhere outdoors with her five children in tow.

Made in United States
North Haven, CT
02 August 2022

22143399R00154